ZenDoodle Patterns and Tangles for Beginners

Start to create your Zen Doodle masterpieces

I0463296

+ 7 Bonus Templates to Incorporate Your Own ZenDoodle Patterns

Betty D. Caton

Table of Contents

Disclaimer

While all attempts have been made to verify the information provided in this book, the author does assume any responsibility for errors, omissions, or contrary interpretations of the subject matter contained within. The information provided in this book is for educational and entertainment purposes only. The reader is responsible for his or her own actions and the author does not accept any responsibilities for any liabilities or damages, real or perceived, resulting from the use of this information.

The trademarks that are used are without any consent, and the publication of the trademark is without permission or backing by the trademark owner. All trademarks and brands within this book are for clarifying purposes only and are the owned by the owners themselves, not affiliated with this document.

Introduction

Welcome to this instructional guide book on both Zen Doodles and the patterns that make them up. In these pages you won't just learn about specific Zen doodles, but also about the Zen doodle patterns that can be used to make any image you want. In these pages exists the creative power to construct almost anything you can imagine. The secrets are written here and need just to be followed and you can utilize them for whatever outlet it is that you need. Whether it is stress related or a creative passion. These Zen doodles and patterns are good for anyone who has the desire to create something. Not only is it fun and relaxing but it's also rather quickly becoming a way of life. A way to exist in the world at a center that can only be found in the most peaceful of places. So utilize that as the inspiration you need to open up this book the rest of the way and get crafting your Zen doodles and patterns. There are a nice and round total of 20 patterns in this book that you will get to explore. I will explain both what it is your looking at and how to achieve the desired image. After those patterns we will dive in to 7 unique and interesting different Zen doodles to see how you can apply the patterns to a full structured image with personal inspiration. Once finished this book you will be a Zen master and a professional Zen doodler. So why wait to dive in and get your journey started. Go on ahead now and crack open the next page. A state of pure calmness and peace awaits you!

Pattern 1

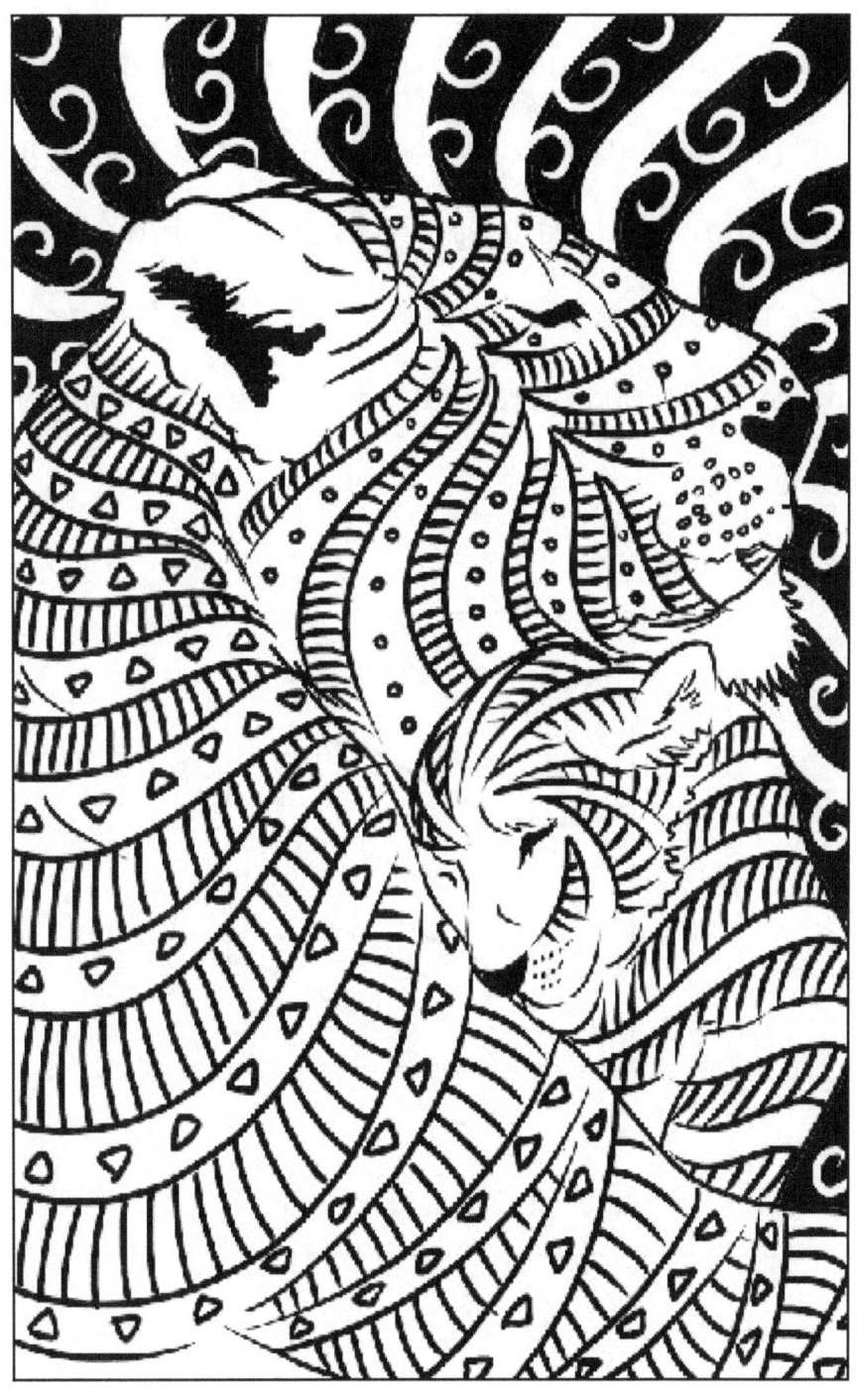

This pattern is our starting place for this book. As you can see it's a wave style pattern that starts incredibly simply then moves on to a more complicated design. You'll want to be careful with your penmanship and watch the lines. The most important thing to keep in mind is the special areas within the wave lines. As well as the dots in between the waves. Spend some time on this pattern and make sure that you got it fully mastered for potential later use.

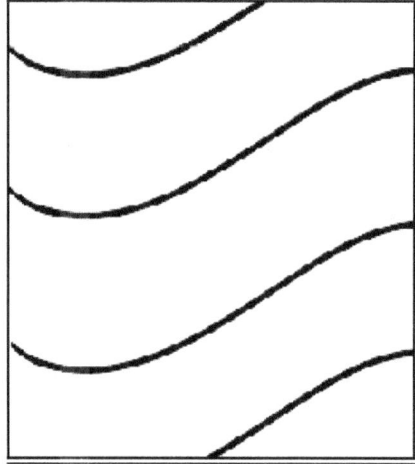

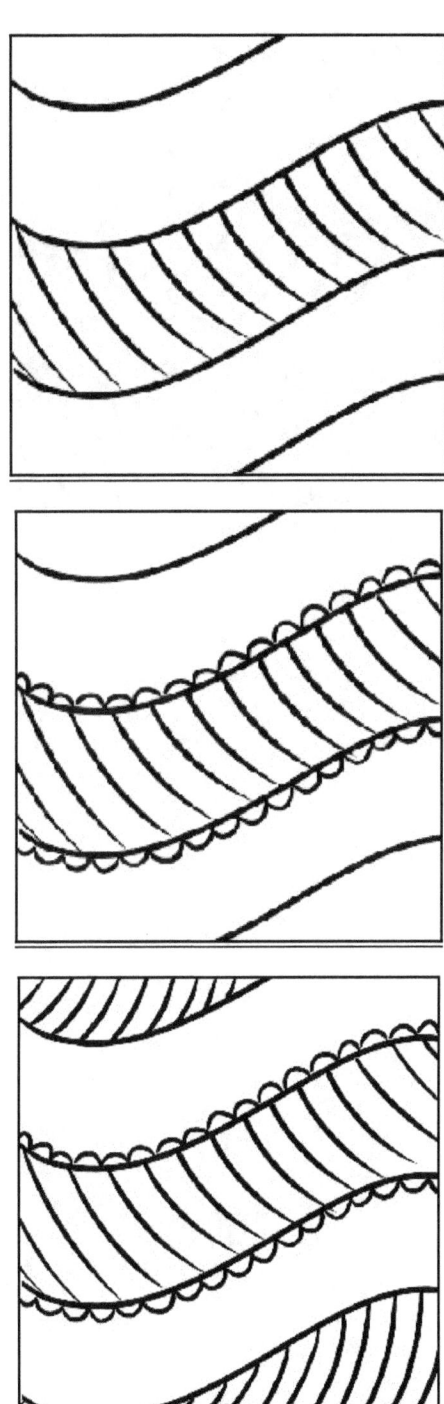

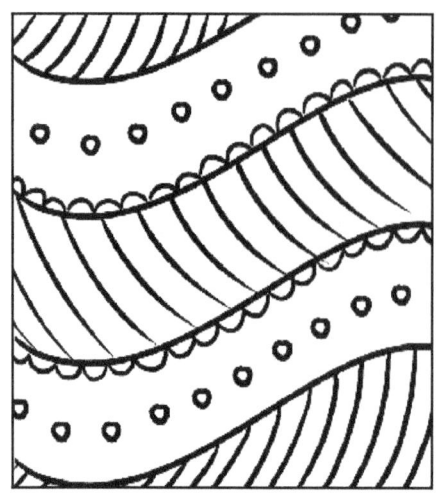

Pattern 2

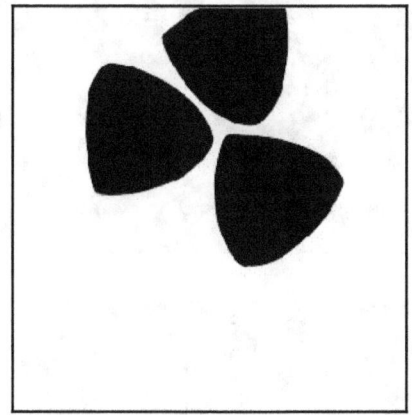

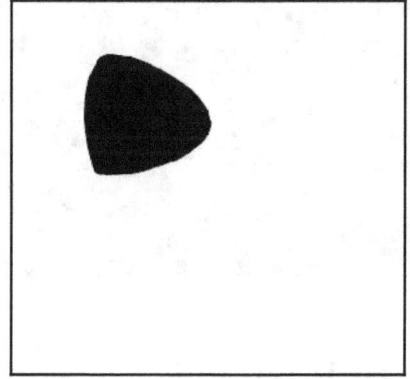

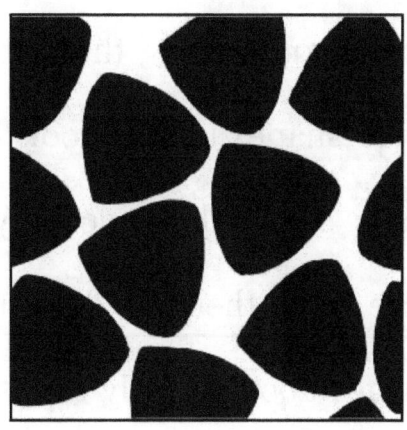

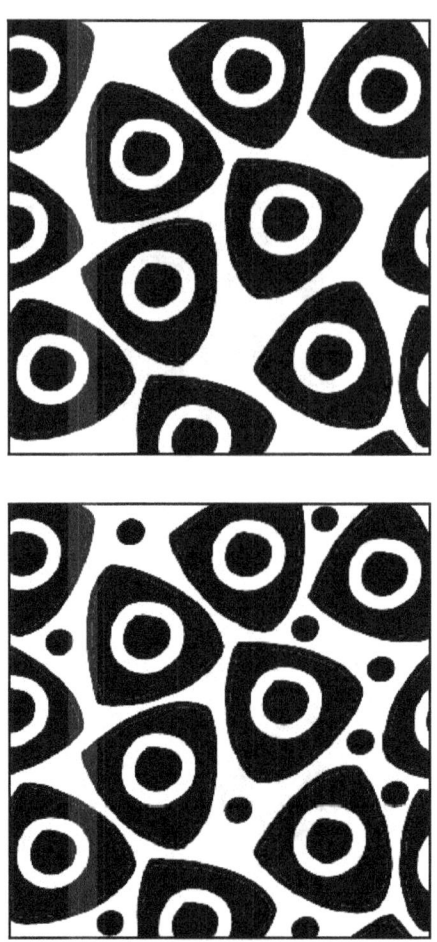

This next pattern is instantly a major departure from the last one we just did. As you can see the feature is a three sided rounded triangle style shape. It may look like there's no real structure to this specific pattern but if you pay close attention you can see that by image three there's a discernible pattern taking hold. Follow the images above closely and see where they take you in the design. Watch the dots in the last image and again get as close to perfect as you're able to while enjoying the work. Then move on to the next pattern once you feel comfortable with your work on this one.

Pattern 3

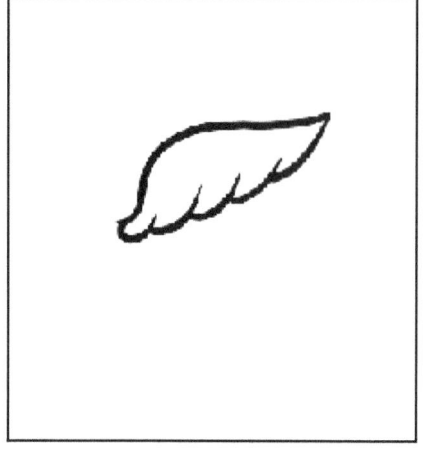

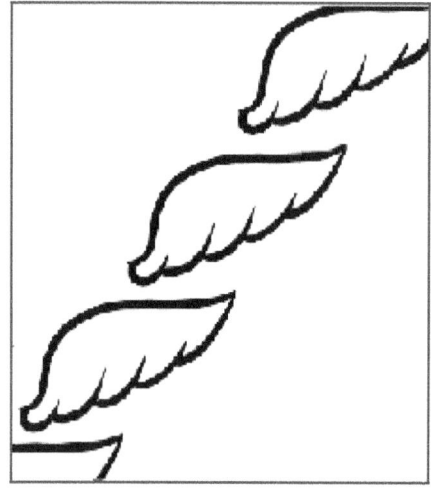

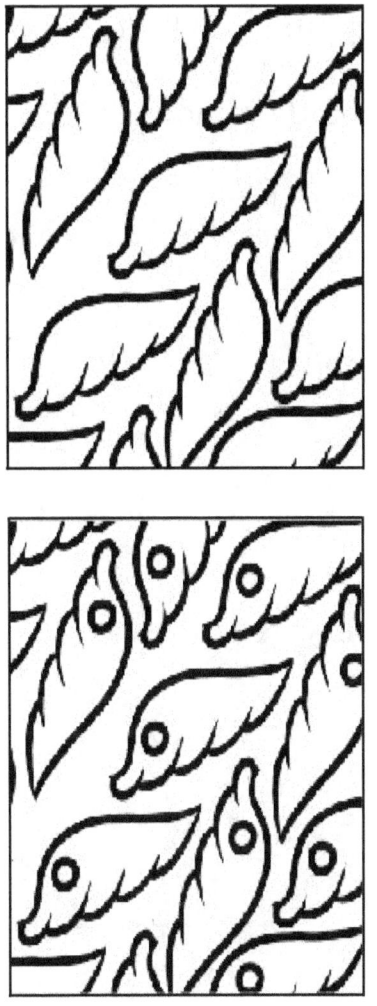

Now we're on to one that's a little more on the adorable

side in my opinion. You've got a sea shell looking image in the

first one, and then you replicate them and create this very

beautiful looking pattern. It's got a nice repetition style to it and

the pattern has a definite style to it that you can't ignore. The

hardest part that you should focus on is lining up the shell images

in a straight line despite not having the line tangibly visible. Pay attention to the lining and you'll do great. Again, practice this pattern a few times and then move on to the next one when you feel as though you're ready!

Pattern 4

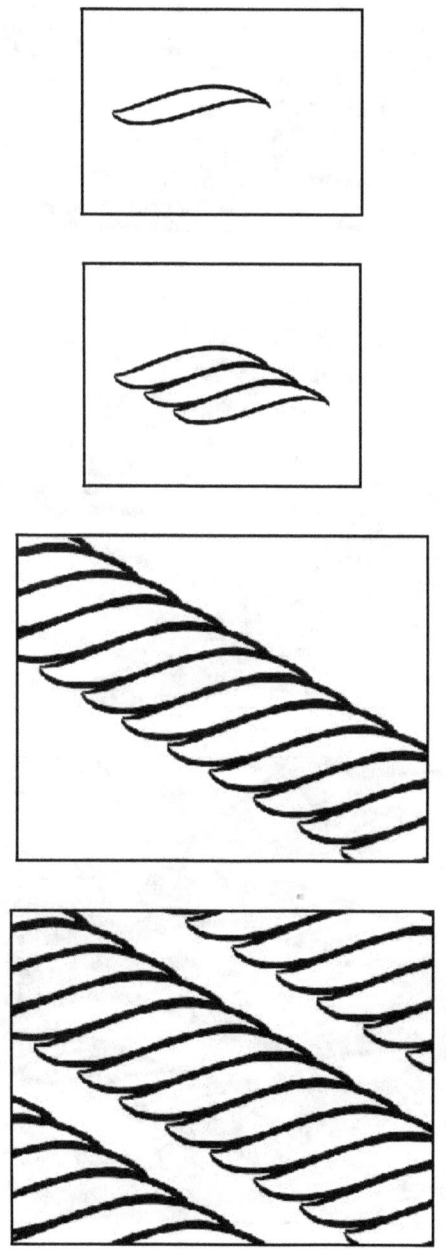

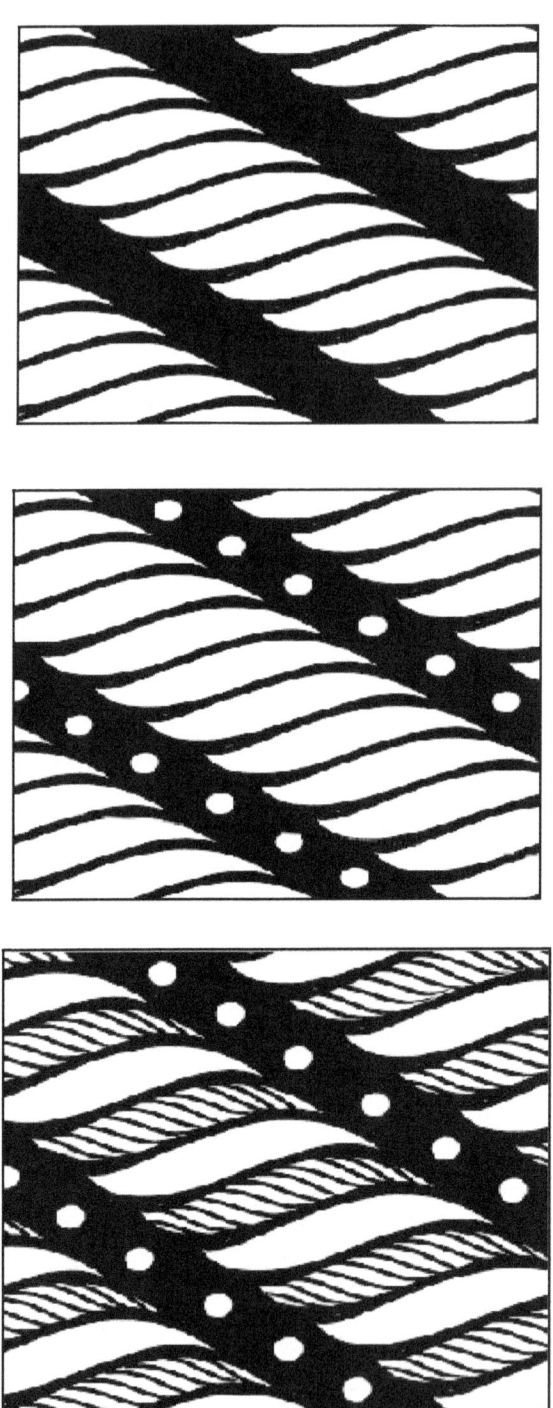

Next up we have a pattern that starts out looking like a feather and ends up looking like a rope. That's pretty impressive if I do say so myself! To start take a good look at the first couple images on the upper left, then slowly make your way all the way to the one on the far right. Try not to get too intimidated by what you see. With focus and patience you'll have yourself an incredible looking pattern in no time at all. Try your best to keep at these patterns and practice them when you can. The doodles to come are a touch complicated and you'll want to be prepared. One last thing, don't forget to have a great time while doing it!

Pattern 5

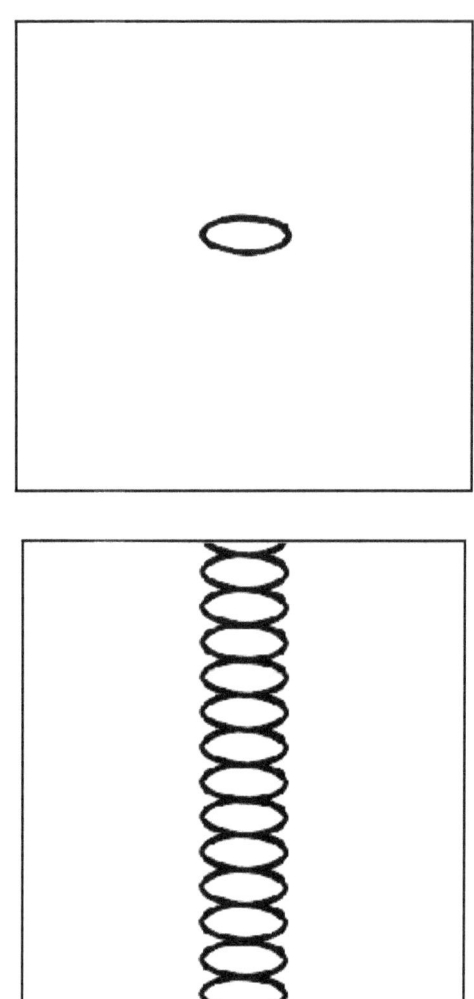

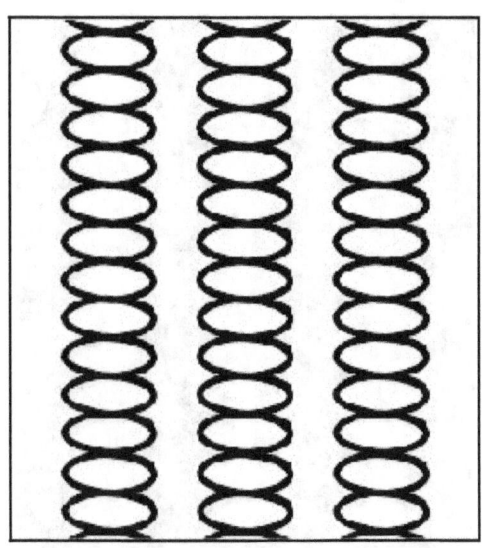

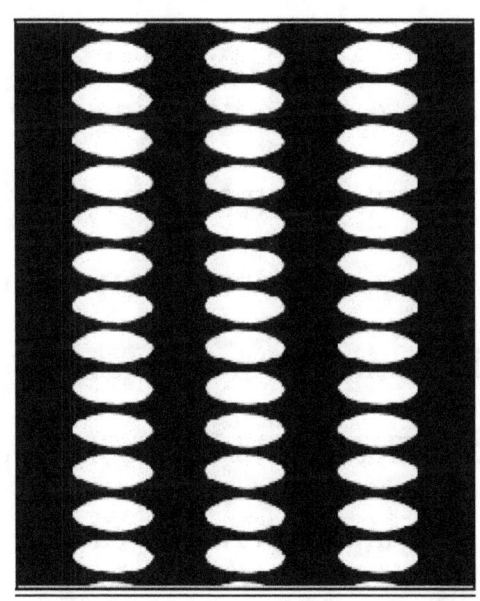

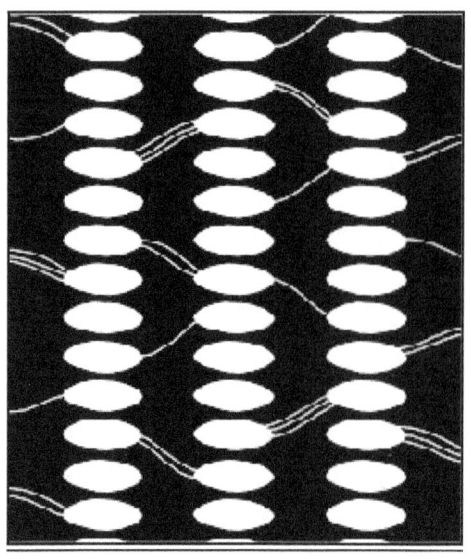

For this pattern we have a flat coin shape to start, and then we're going to stack them on top of each other from top of image to bottom. Then we triple the stacks and then it's time to start shading! Shading is the most important aspect of this pattern but not the most critical. That would be the line work required after the actual shading is completed. As you can see in the final image you have a very intricate sort of line work marked into the shading. It is definitely something that needs to be done post shading, in case you were curious. Try your hand at this one; I know you can do your best! Then when you're ready, proceed on to the next pattern to further hone your skills in preparation of the doodles.

Pattern 6

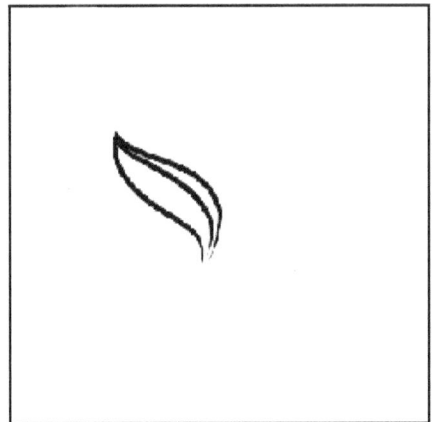

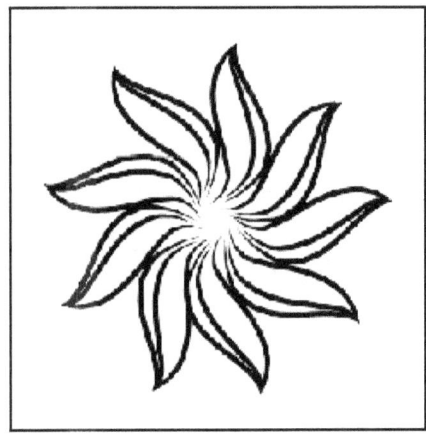

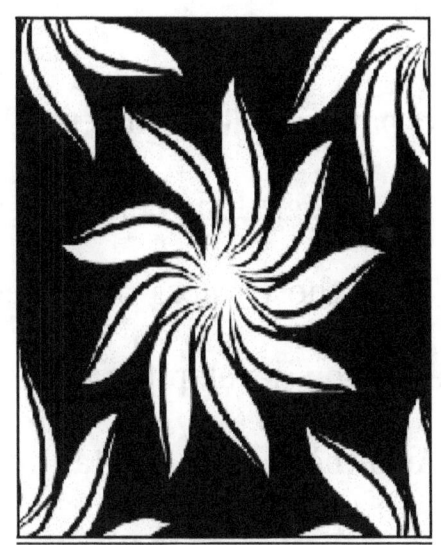

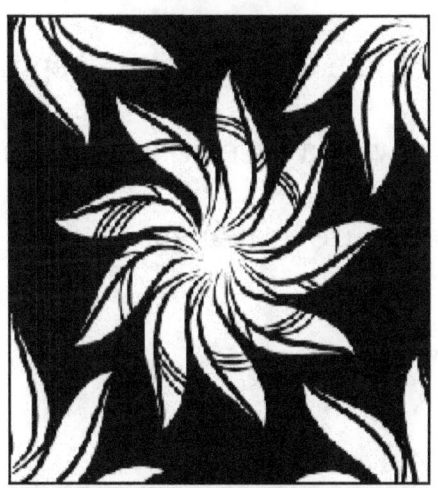

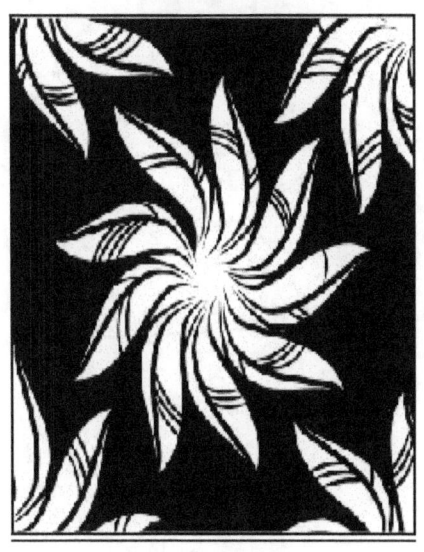

On to this next pattern with a nice petal flower pattern. As you can see the start is a single lone petal, but it grows from there into a full flower. Then the corners have developed flowers as well. As you can see, as you develop the pattern you shade in the background again. Also the most important part of the design is the details on the petals. You'll see that they develop through the last three images on the bottom. If you keep the pattern nice and clean you'll come up with a nice crisp pattern that you can learn and take to heart for future drawings.

Pattern 7

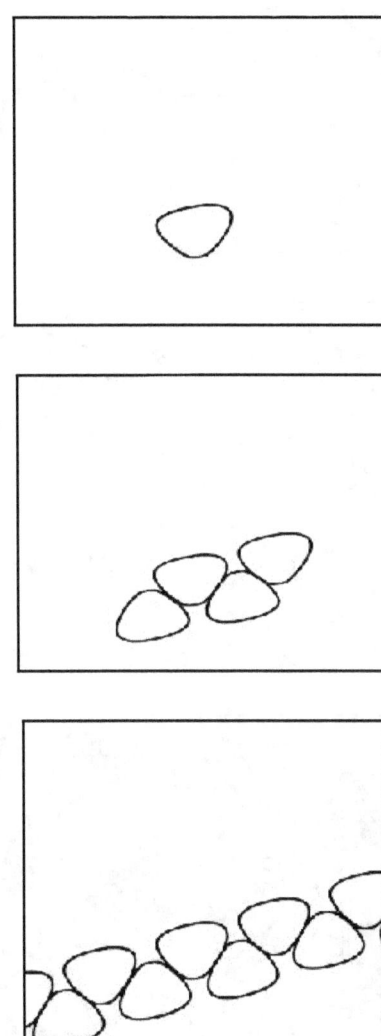

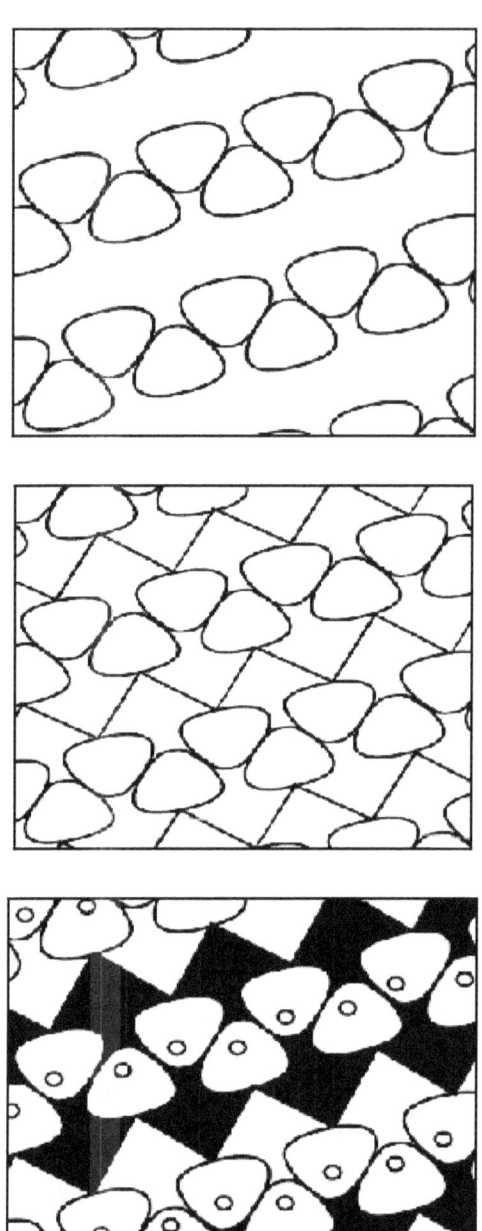

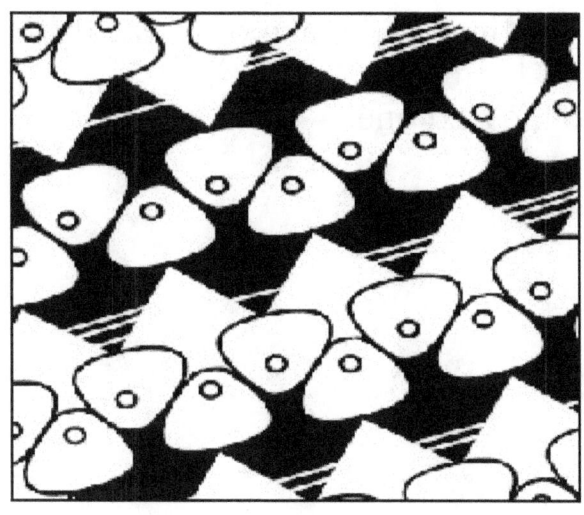

Now for this one we see something different all over again, something we haven't quite come across yet. It's a lot like a chain pattern although there are some very important intricacies to pay attention to and keep in mind. For starters the links of the chain don't actually interlock or link at all. As well as that there are small circles in them as seen in the last two images. Also, there are triangle shapes in between each set of chain links. The shading is as well every important here just like the details in the triangle shapes. Take your time with the actual links as well as the line work after that. The biggest mistake you can make on any of these patterns is to rush through them in order to finish quicker. Take your time, and make your way through this pattern then move on to the next one.

Pattern 8

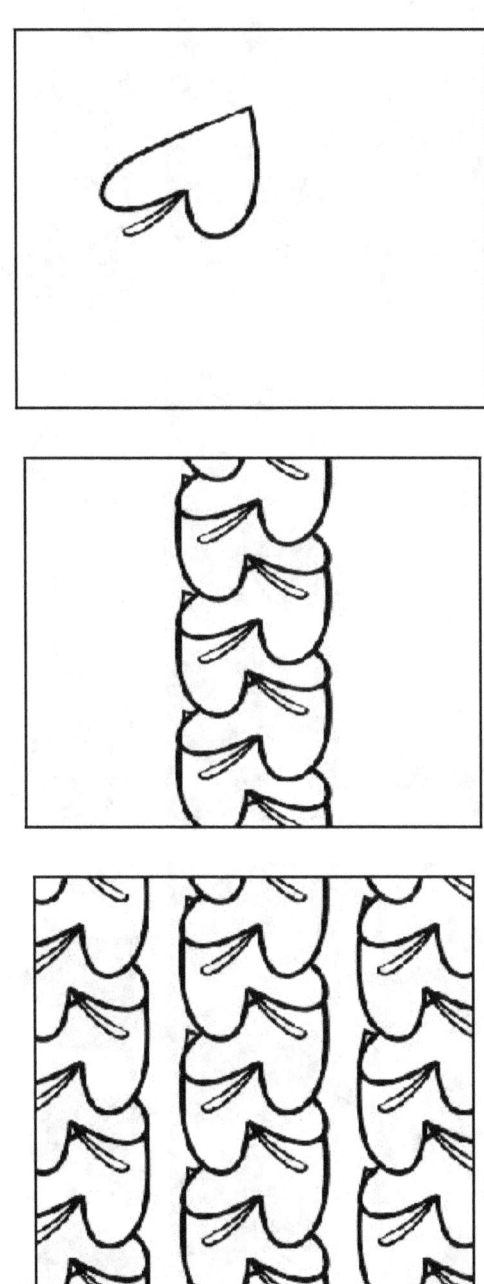

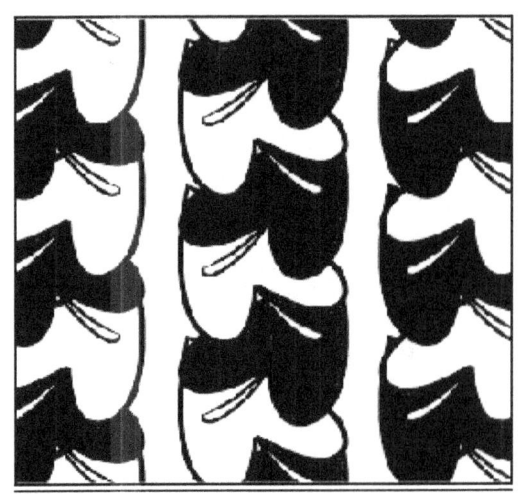

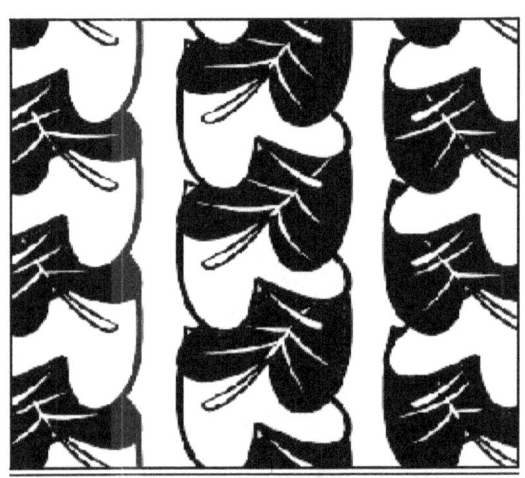

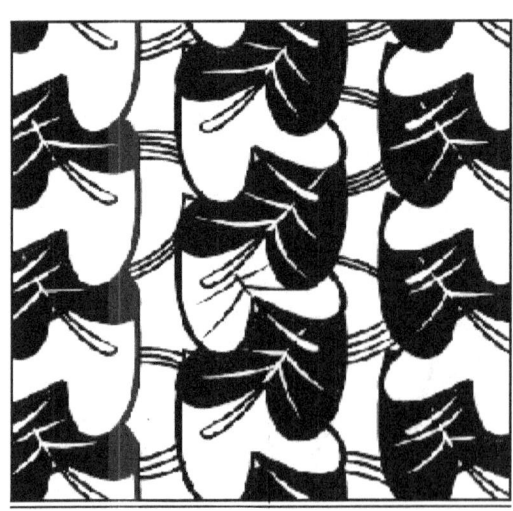

Now for this one we see a pattern based solely on repetition of the original image. A leaf is replicated numerous times to create the beautiful pattern you see on the bottom right image. As you can also see the images alternate between black and white shades. You can do something similar to that in any pattern you wish, for this one it's very crucial that you follow it implicitly. As well as that you need to pay close attention to the markings on the individual leaves when you're crafting them so as to make a nice and neat image. Keep your lines sharp and straight as well as your curves polished and smooth and you shouldn't have a single issue with your patterns. Keep up the good work and proceed to the next pattern!

Pattern 9

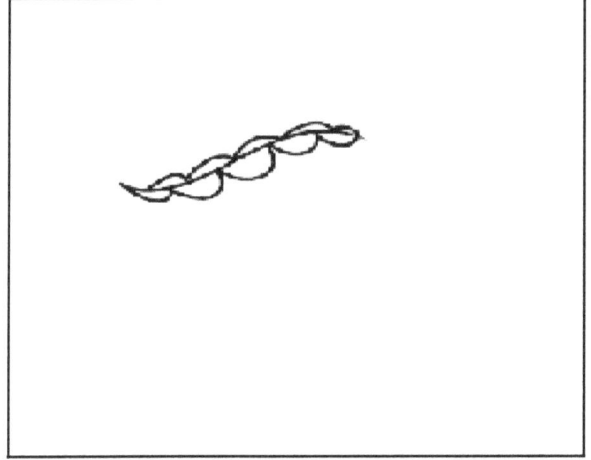

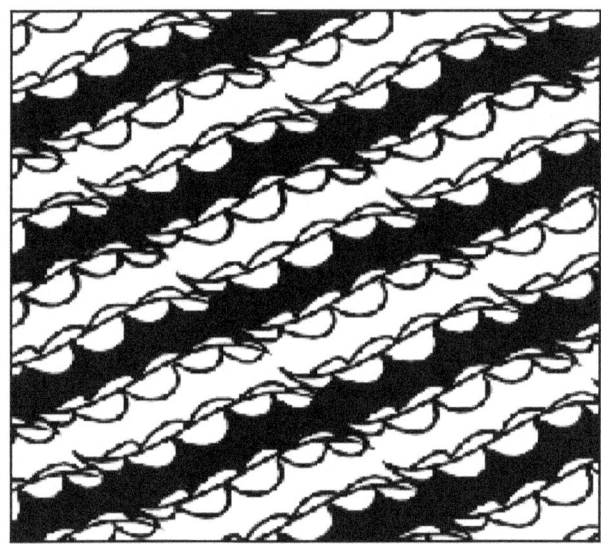

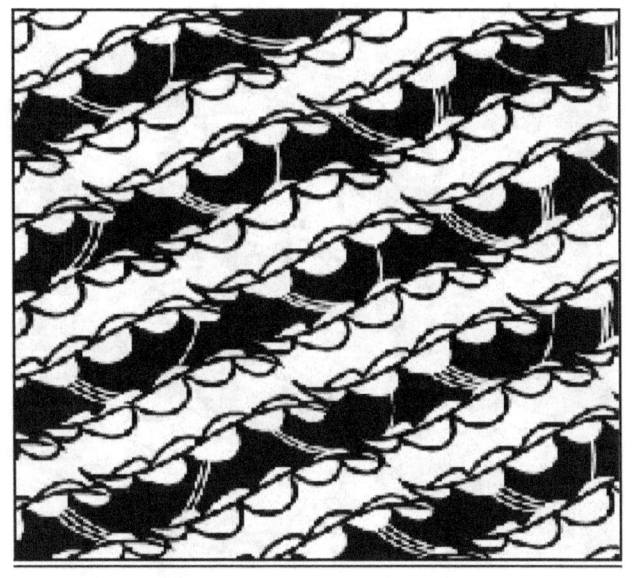

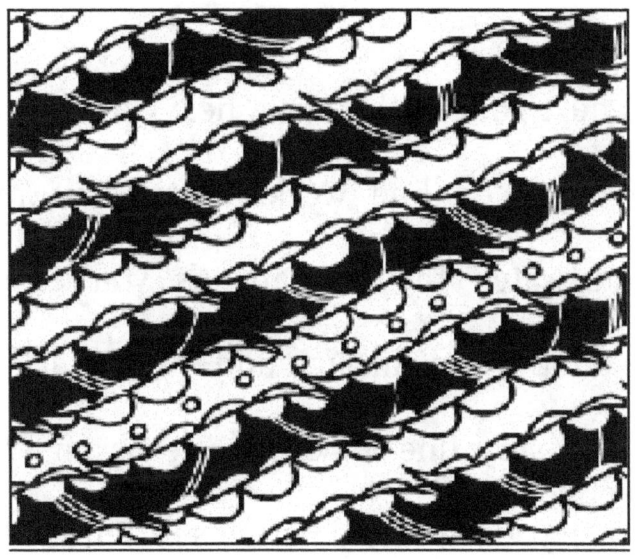

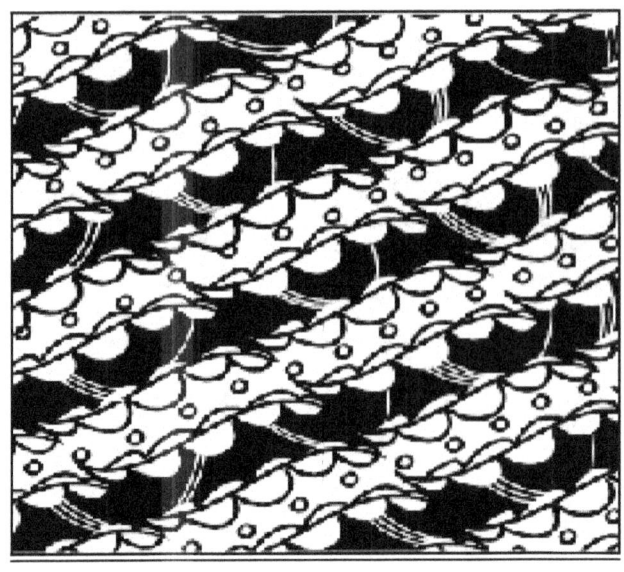

For this next pattern there is a heavy focus on the shading as well as the curved line work. Watch out for the slight intricacies and watch the overlap. As you've noticed these patterns have a lot of run through and overlap, if done correctly you'll have some very fine looking patterns on your hands so make sure to take your time and pay close attention to the lines!

Pattern 10

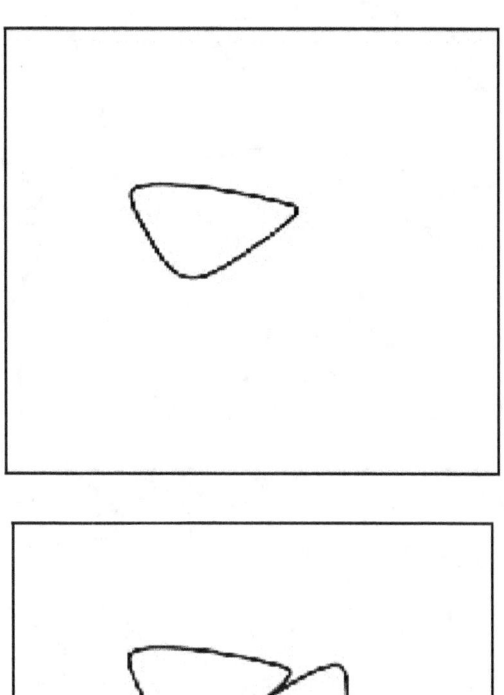

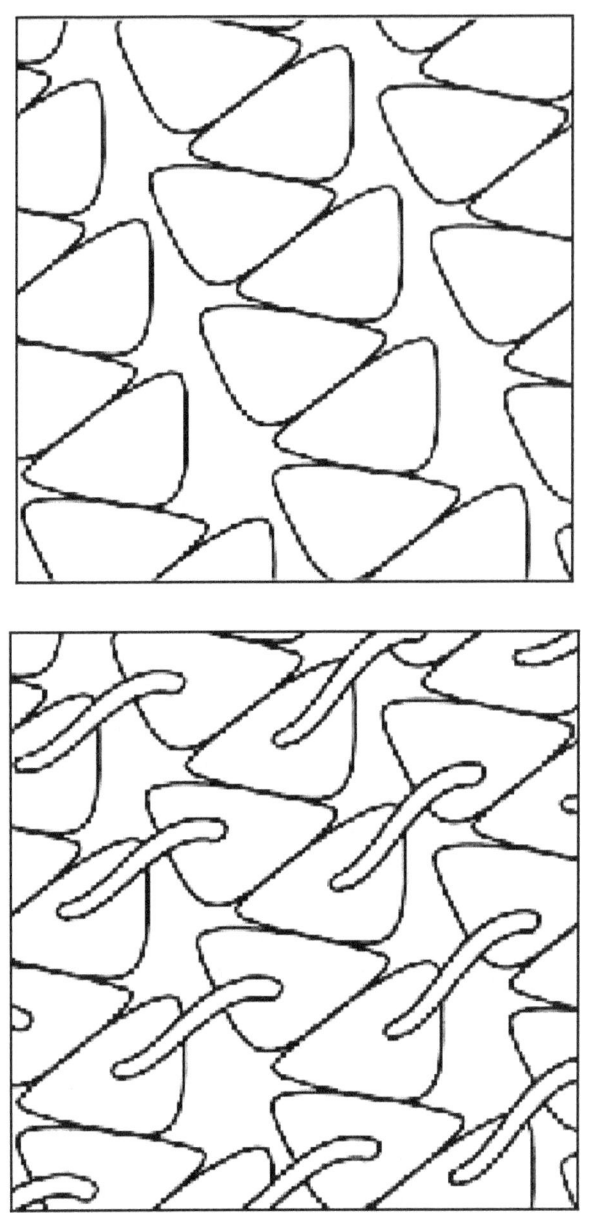

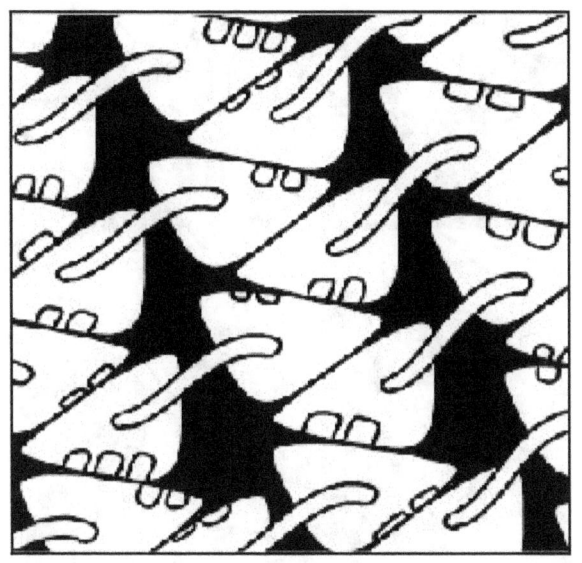

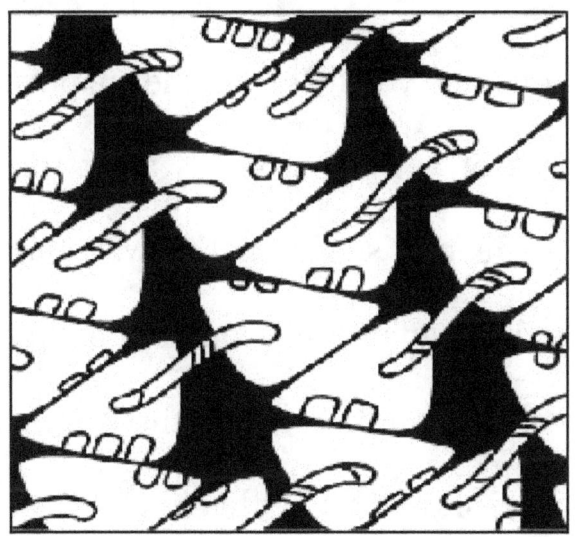

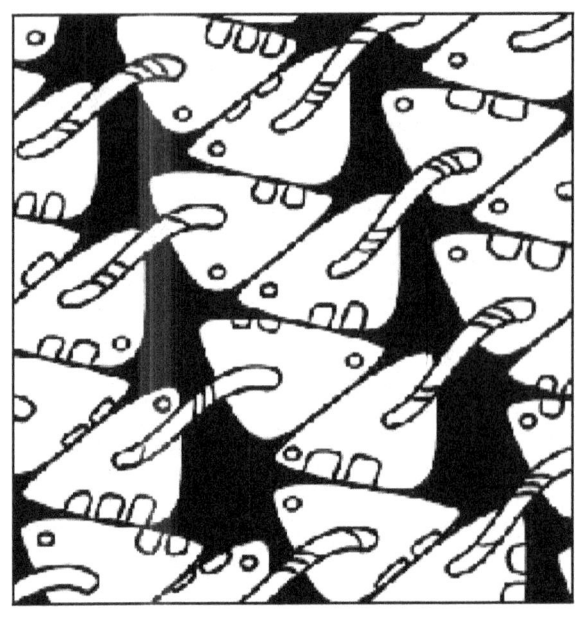

Now with this one you'll see another major difference from the other patterns of yet. This one is a lot more strange and unique looking. You can see it in the way the shapes are all connected above the shaded background in the last image. So get started with the shapes and line work, then connect the, shade it in and add the details. It won't be that complex once you actually get started and manage to get a solid grip on the patterns difficulties. One recommendation I would have is to make sure that you watch the line work on each individual shape and how they are interconnected with the other shapes. Every detail is important so be sure to not overlook any aspect of the pattern.

Pattern 11

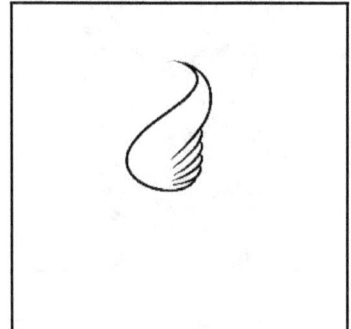

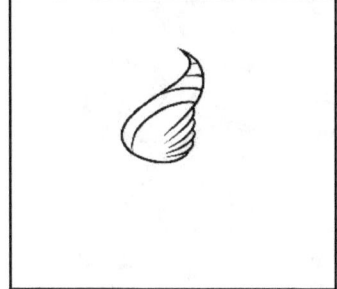

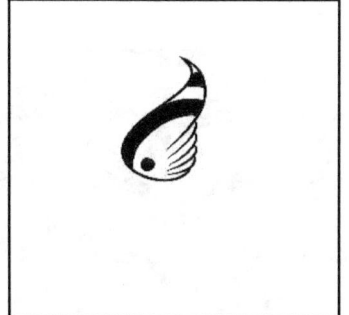

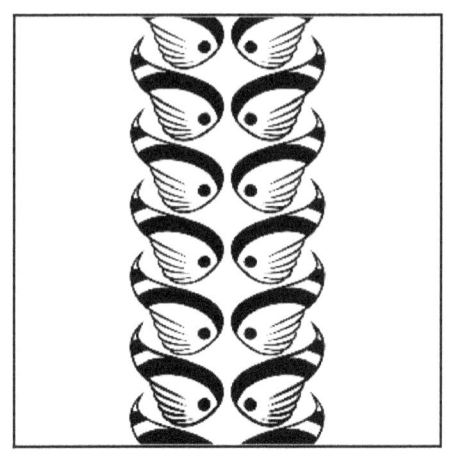

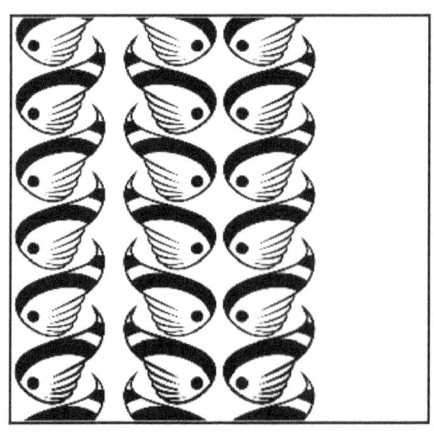

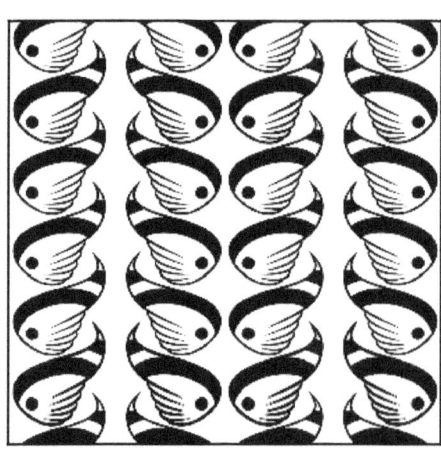

On to this pattern that has a very specific and interesting

design to it. This pattern is a very simple start and a fairly basic follow through in the design. As you see, it's a very gradual escalation starting with a basic shape with simple design. Them you add a few details and some light shading, and then you replicate the image to craft a very beautiful and fulfilling pattern. If you master this pattern then you're already over halfway through learning all the patterns in this book! Move on to the next pattern and keep this guy in your back pocket.

Pattern 12

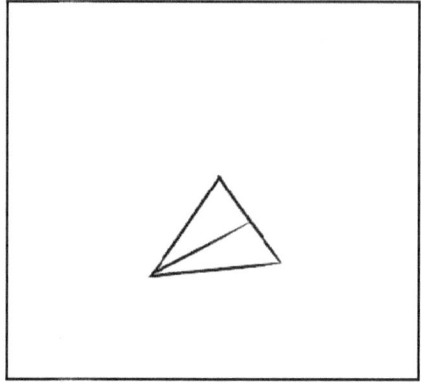

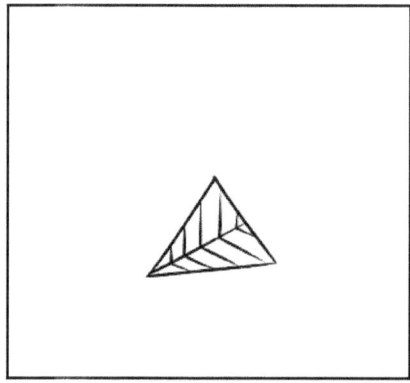

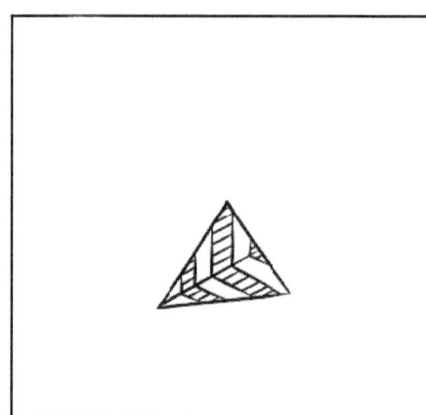

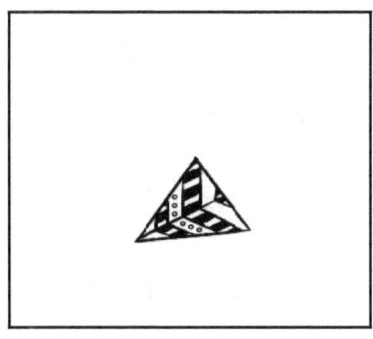

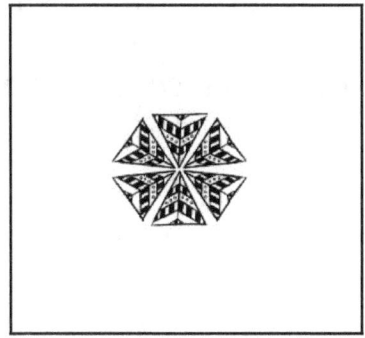

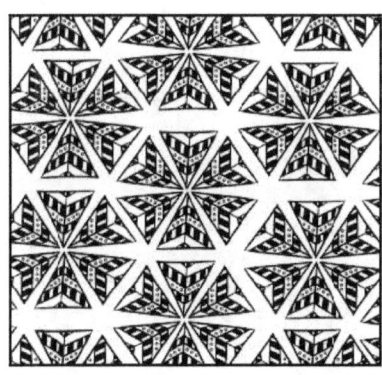

Now this pattern again comes as a pleasant surprise in the line of patterns we've been working on. It starts out as just a simple image and then becomes so much more as you elaborate on it. Add the intricacies carefully as you expand on its design. As you see in the fourth image the shading becomes a very important part of the design. Then the whole pattern takes a turn for the unique in the next image when you replicate the shape you just made in a hexagon style. Then you simply replicate that again and again to create your unique and extravagant pattern! The key to a pattern with this style is to really closely craft the initial image and then the actual construction of the replication is much easier.

Pattern 13

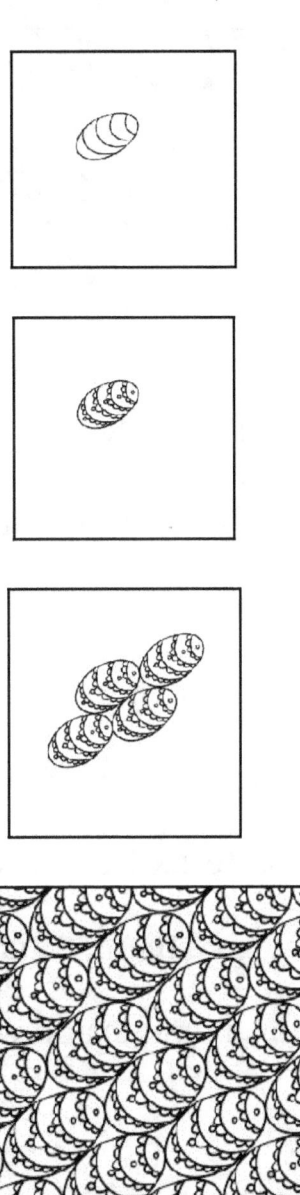

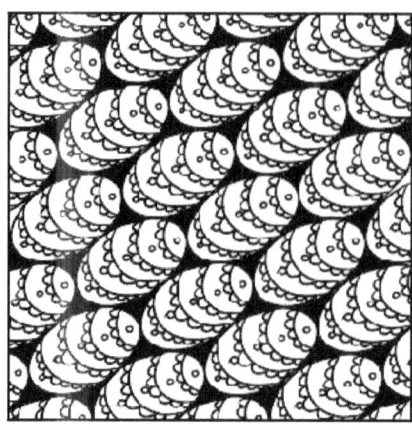

As with the last pattern, this one focuses a great deal on the replication of a singularly intricate shape. A major difference however is the shading between all of the finished images. As you'll notice there is a very distinct change in look between the shaded image and the non-shaded image. That is always a nice way to separate your patterns from one another should you be looking for a way to enhance them. A bit of shading can go a long way when you're crafting a unique and wonderful pattern?

Pattern 14

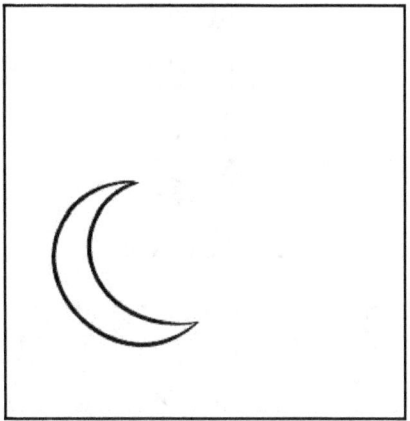

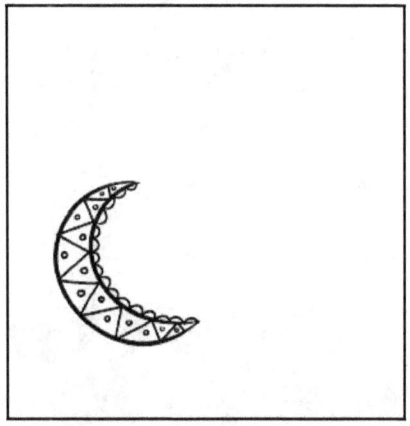

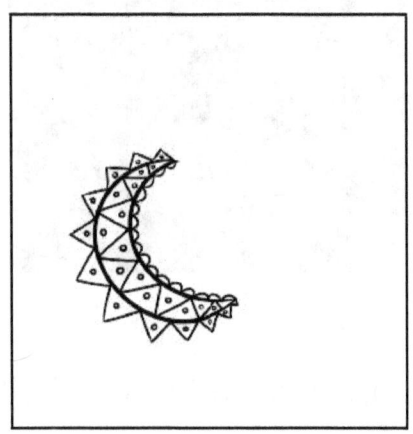

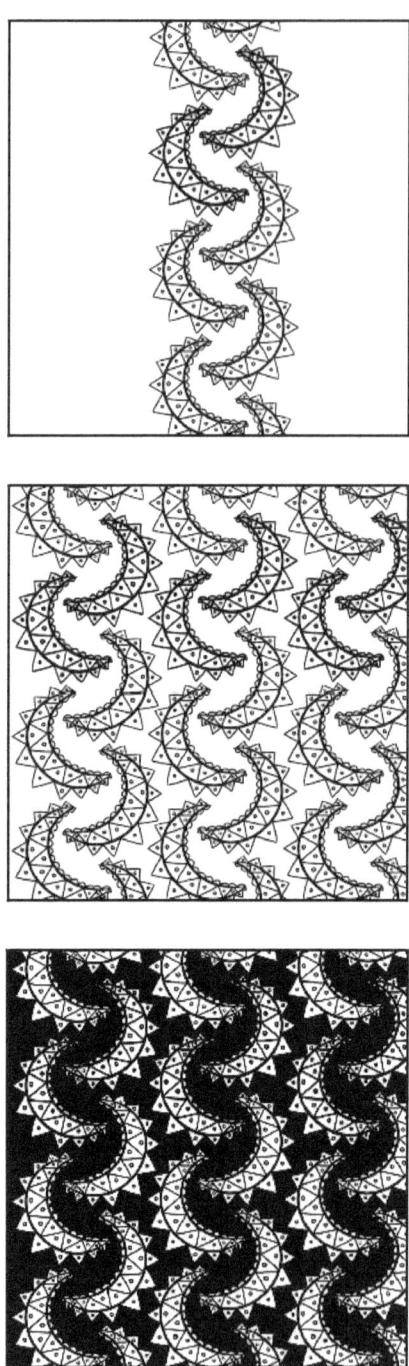

Again we have a pattern a lot like the last two. The major

differences here with this one are the many small and minuscule details on the shape itself. This may in fact be the most taxing design yet, with how small a lot of the specific details are. The thing to remember is to not get overwhelmed with them but to focus on each individual line. Then as with the last pattern there's a level of shading required to finish it off and give it a certain level of polish. One of the best methods to making sure that your shading is done right is to compare it with your previous work. Don't hesitate to try out a few different methods when perfecting your work.

Pattern 15

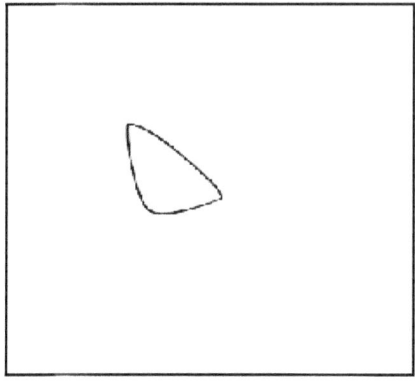

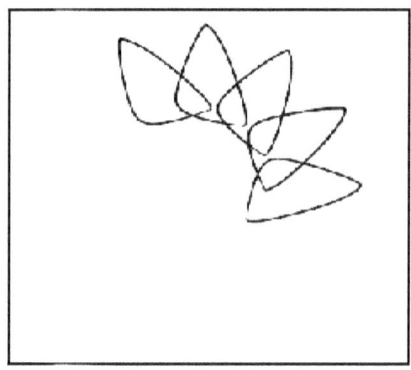

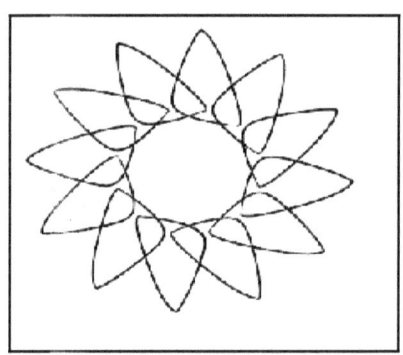

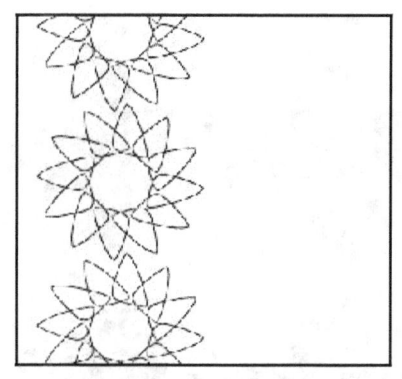

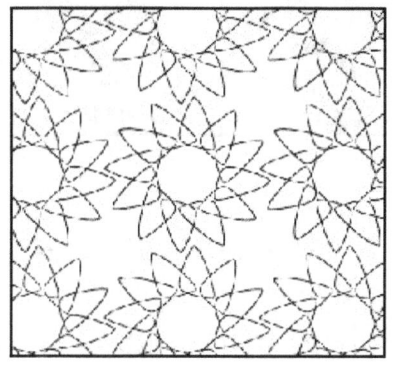

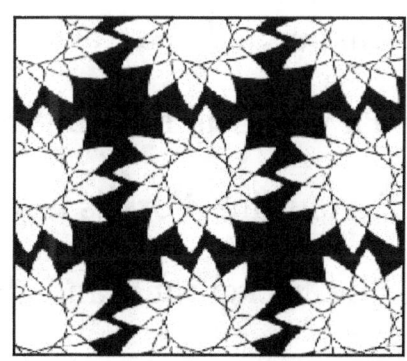

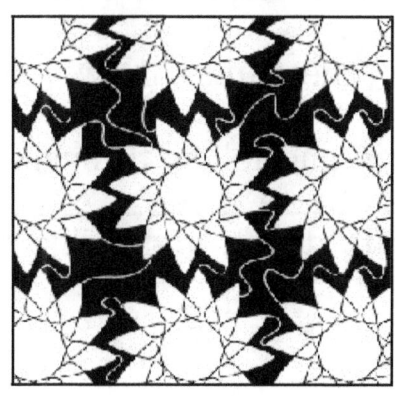

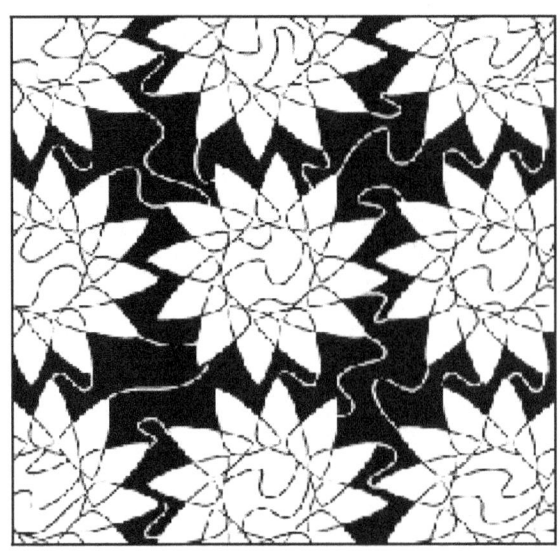

Now we're on to some complex stuff. This pattern is very elaborate but definitely starts simple. As you see the pattern starts with a simple shape, and then a lot of overlap with the same shape. What you'll want will resemble a flower or a sun. As you do this make sure your line work is as accurate as possible. As you go, shade in the background and then prepare for the incredible line work afterword. Trace the lines in through the flower or sun shapes. These lines are wavy so make sure to pay attention to your form and follow through. Pat yourself on the back for this elaborate design and utilize this pattern for the future.

Pattern 16

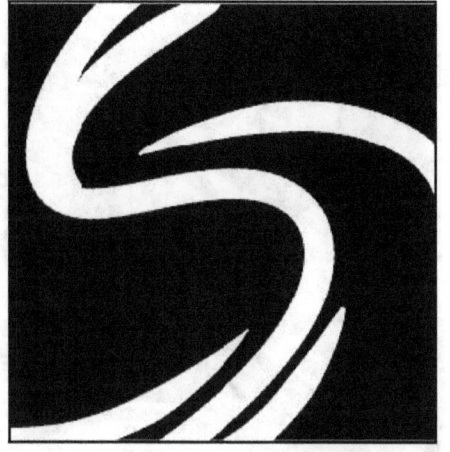

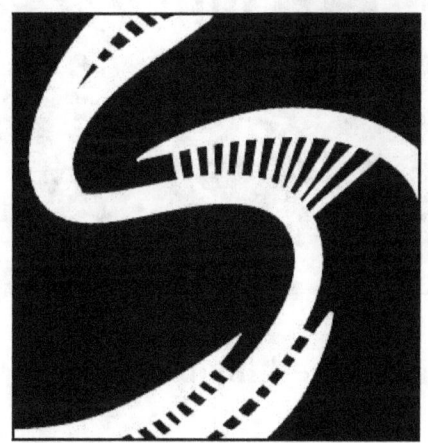

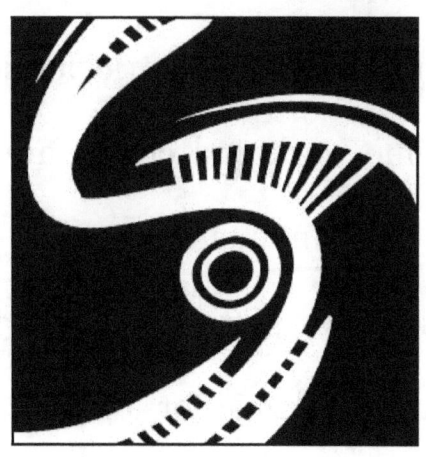

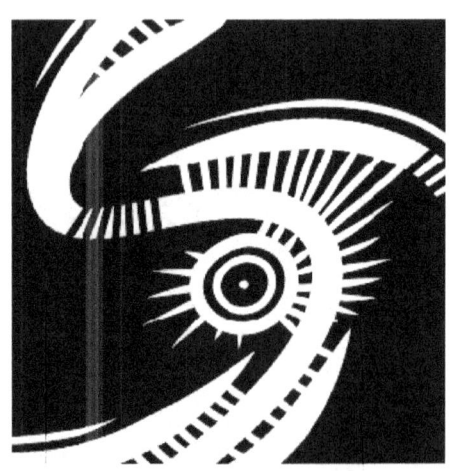

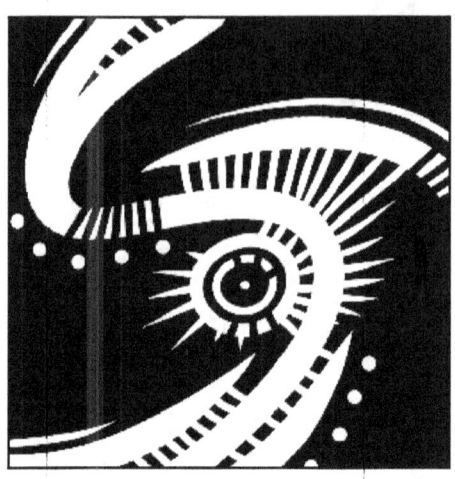

Up now we have something pretty fantastical. We start fully shaded in with very space like lines. Make sure you keep your lines clean and then move on to the trickier details. The addition goes the stitching line work and circles are important. Follow along the images as seen and make sure that you keep it as clean and focused as possible. A pattern like this is harder to use in smaller projects but is fantastic for a bigger project. Enjoy this pattern and move on to the next one when you feel as though you're ready.

Pattern 17

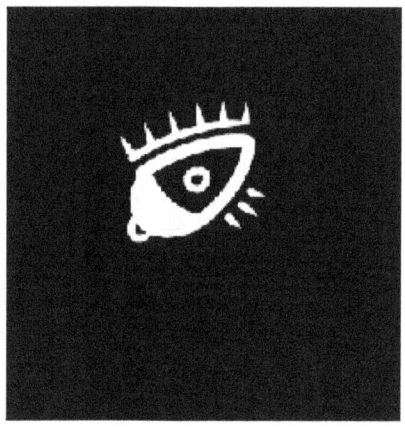

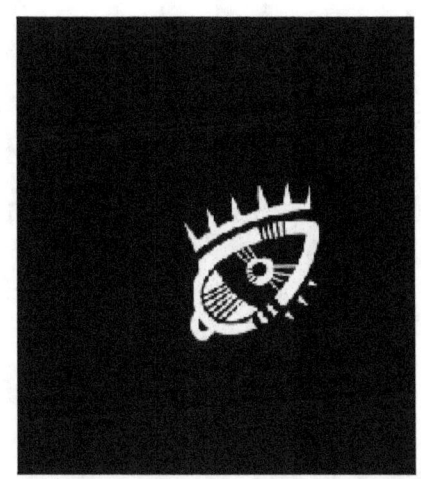

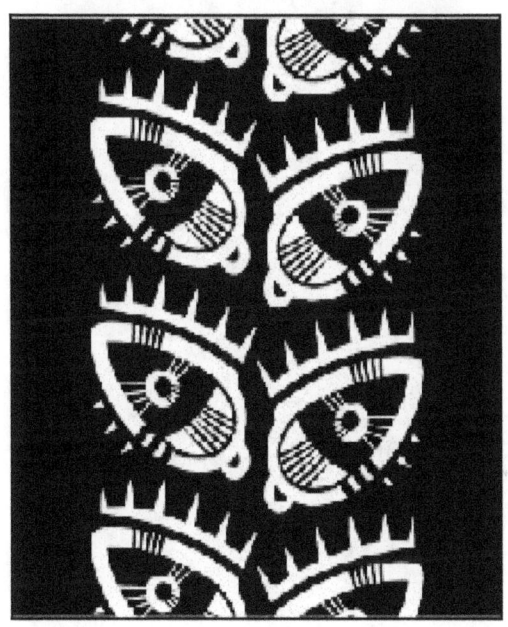

This next pattern is another departure from the usual. We start out with a blacked out background in the first image. The next image, you'll want to start on the pattern and make sure that you get it in proper order. There are a lot of slight and small delicate intricacies that you have to pay close attention to. The focus you should have on the center of the eye is pretty important; there are a lot of small details. Replicate the main image in the final image to get a solid pattern with a very elegant finish.

Pattern 18

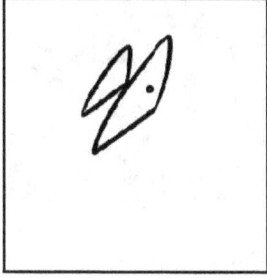

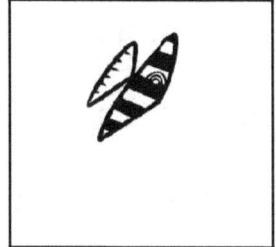

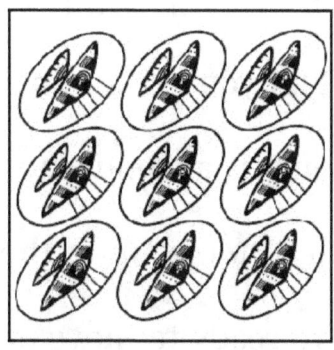

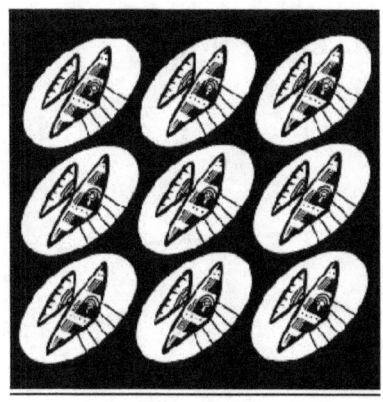

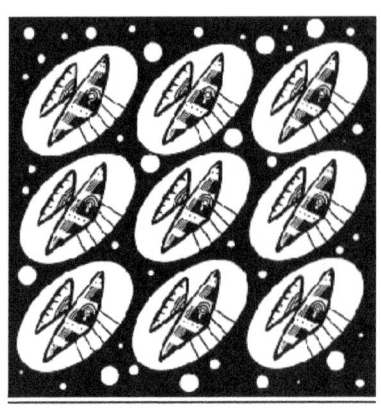

This pattern is particularly interesting. You start out with a simple fish like image, add some shading and a few delicate details, and then you turn it into something else entirely. Circle the images after you fine tune the shading and add a few more details. Display the image in a 3 by 3 pattern and then shade in the background. After that you add in bubbles and the pattern is finished. The final product is a wonderful image and you can do whatever you want with it. Move on to the next pattern and you have two left until you're ready to move on to the doodles. Good job on the work so far! Keep it up.

Pattern 19

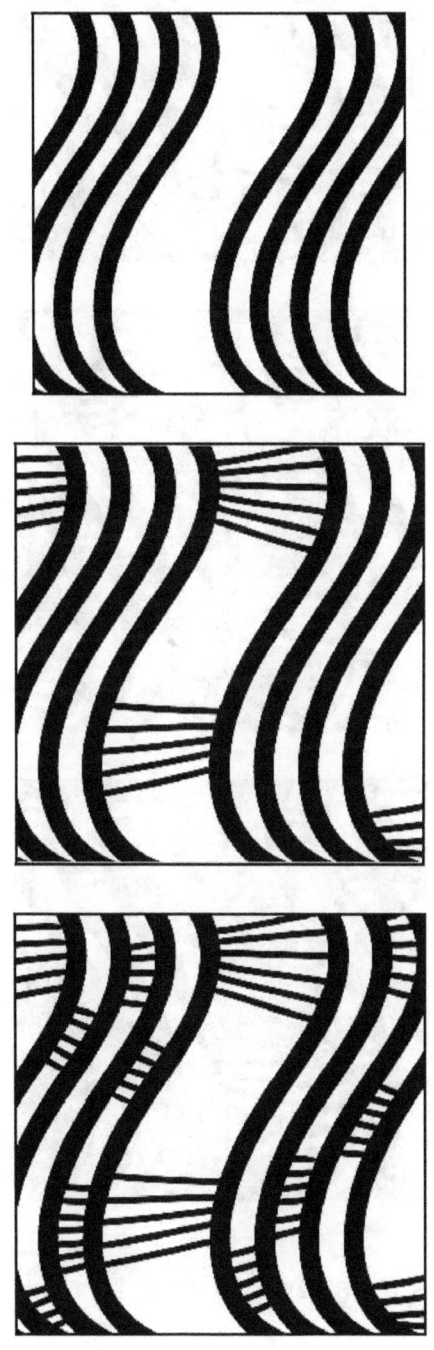

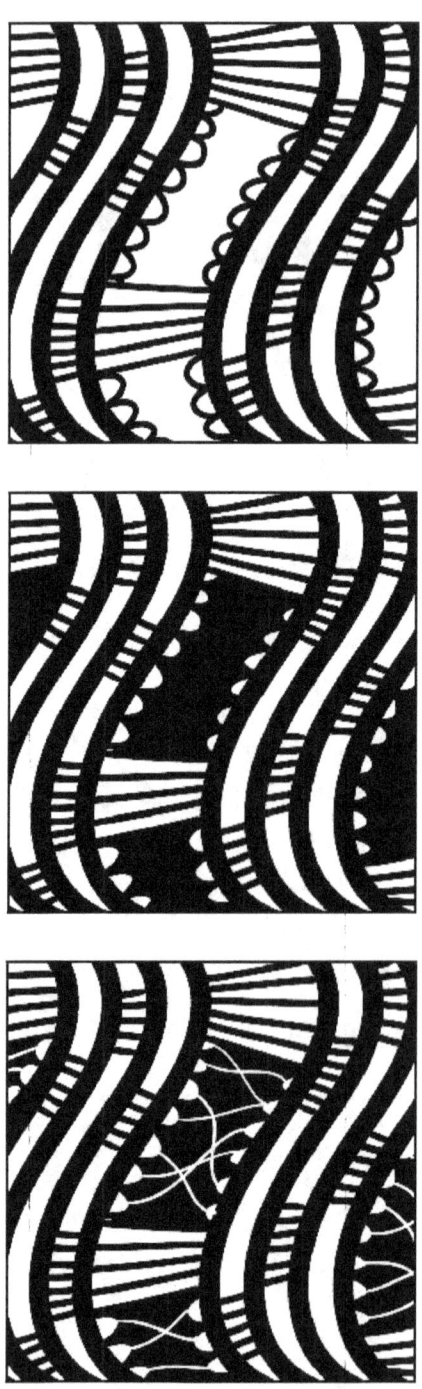

This pattern is a really fun one to do. Start out with thick

solid wavy lines from the top to the bottom of the square. Then connect them with straight lines across, and then add some curved lines and then you'll have to start shading in the empty spaces. As you'll see you have to connect the curved lines in the last image to complete the pattern. This may be an intimidating one if you gauge it by the final image but the reality is that it's all a work of progress and you'll have a good time with it. Keep the pattern working and then move on to the final pattern in the collection.

Pattern 20

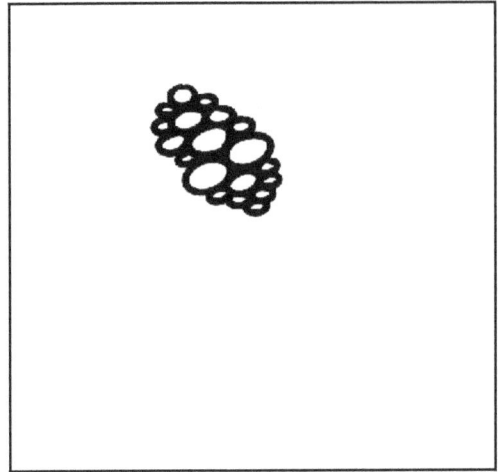

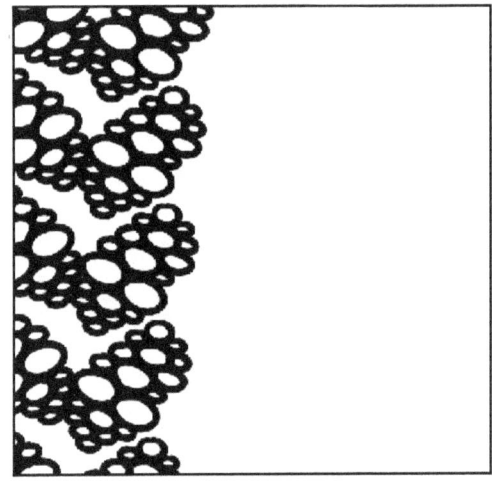

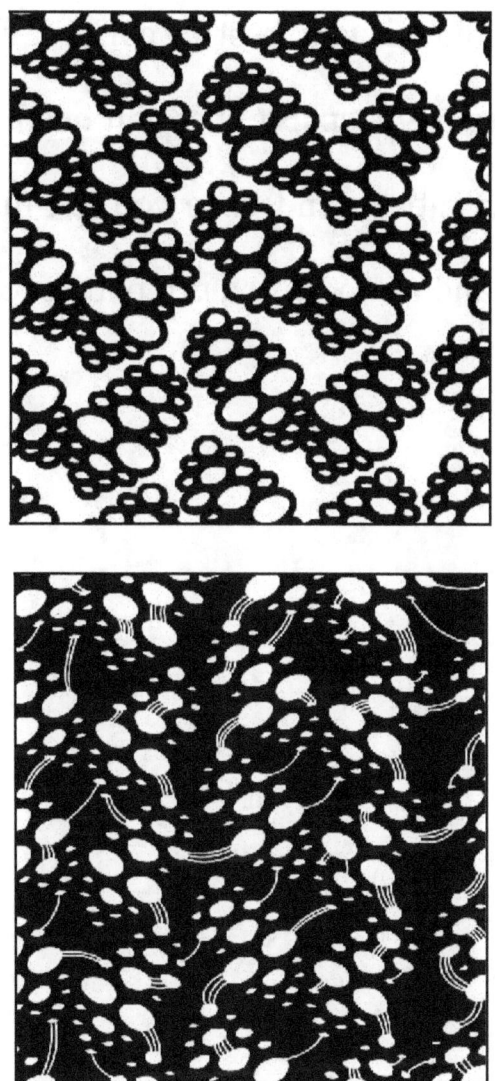

The final pattern of the series is a complex one to finish but it's fairly easy to start. It's like a bunch of grapes in the beginning and then you replicate that image over and over again. Fill the square with that and then shade in the background. The trick here now is that the final image is going to be a lot different than what you start with. Do your best to connect the lines that you need and fill in the blank spaces that you need. You will have no problem with this pattern and once you're finished you'll move on to the doodles and now you're a pro pattern crafter.

Doodle 1 - Lion & Cub

As you can see, we are just going to dive straight into the doodles. We start off with a lion and its cub. The line work to start as seen above is very simple yet detailed and gives the image itself a great starting point for us to look at and visualize the next few steps. Keep that in mind whenever you start a project. Not just where it begins but also where it could end. It will almost always assuredly surprise you. Take a look at the photos just below this as you continue forward and watch how the details expand rather rapidly.

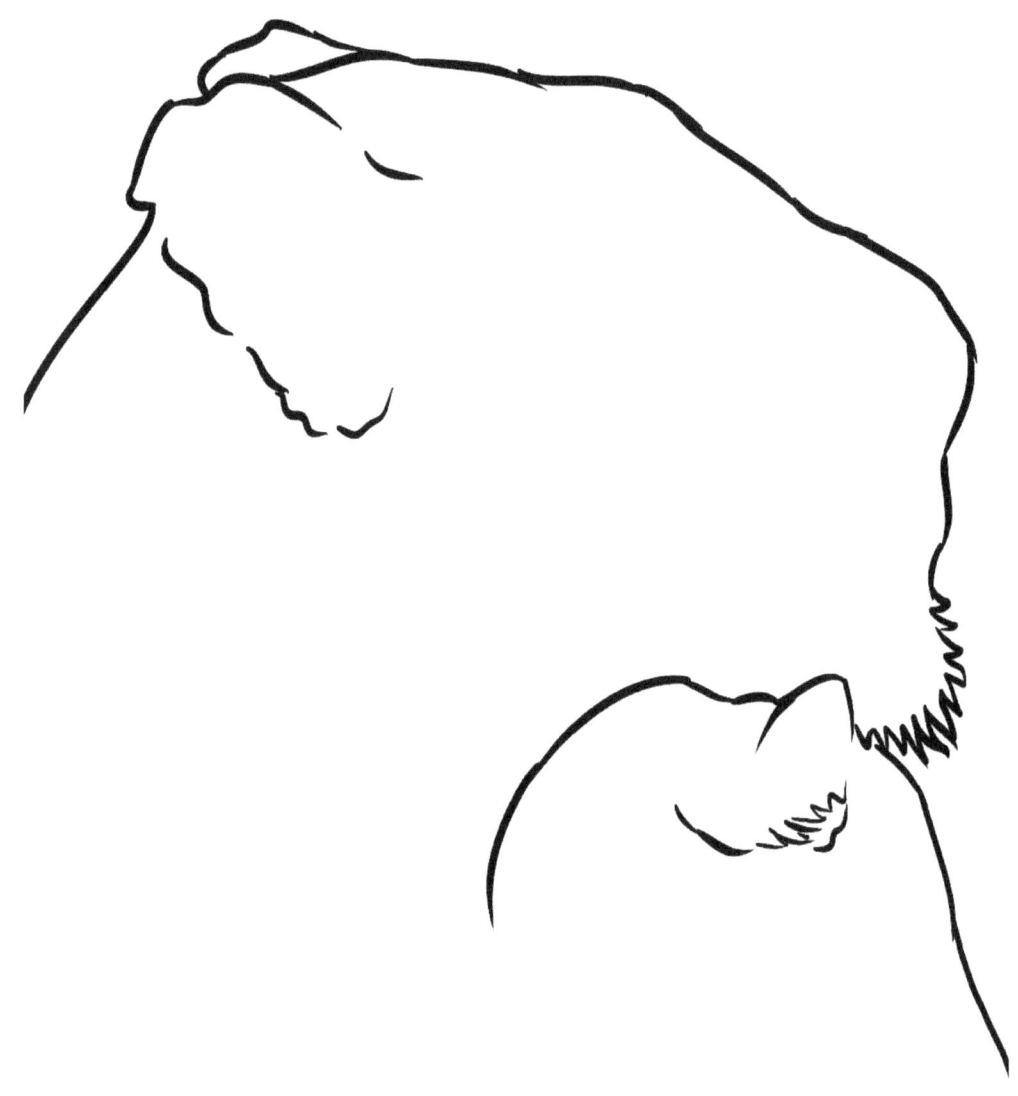

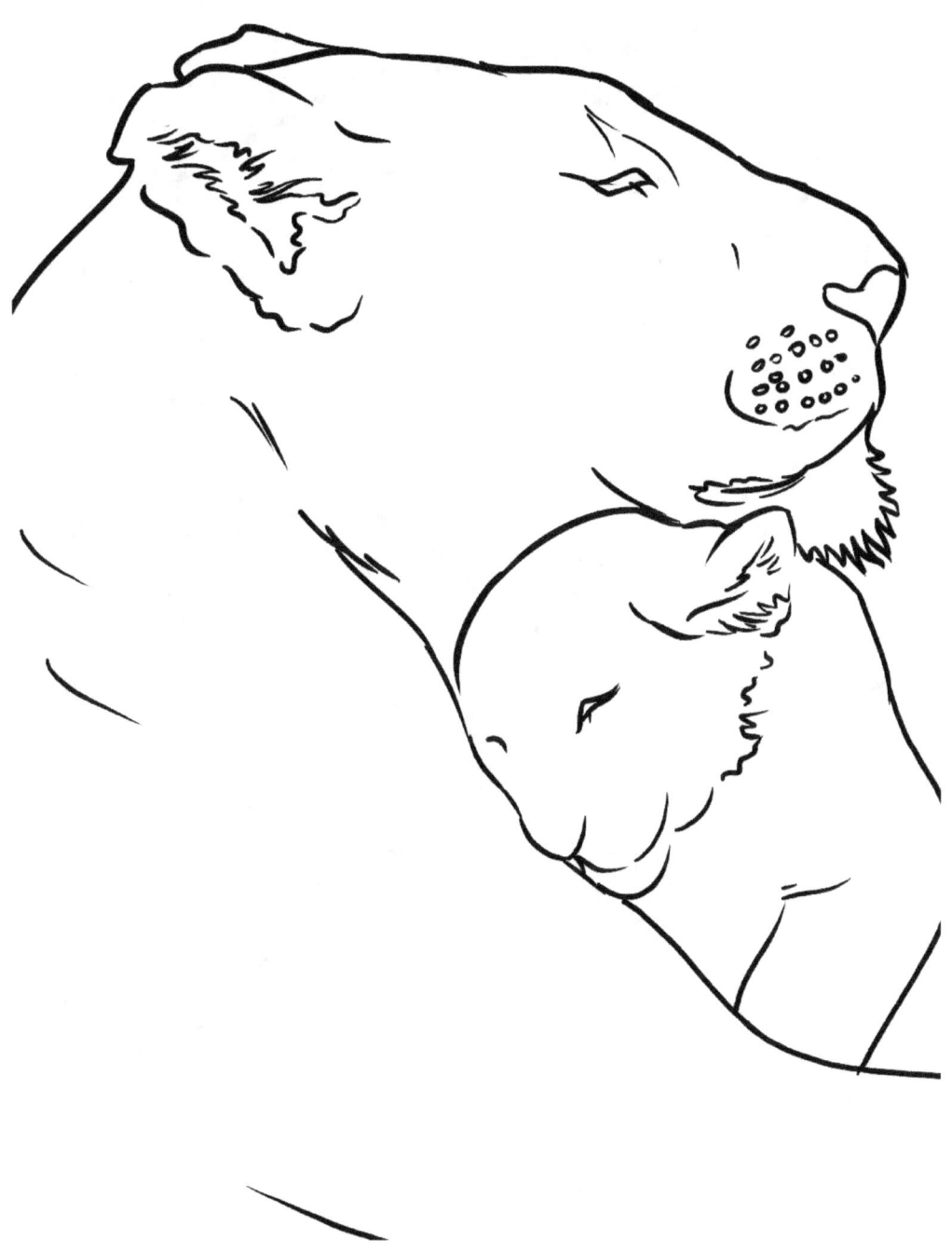

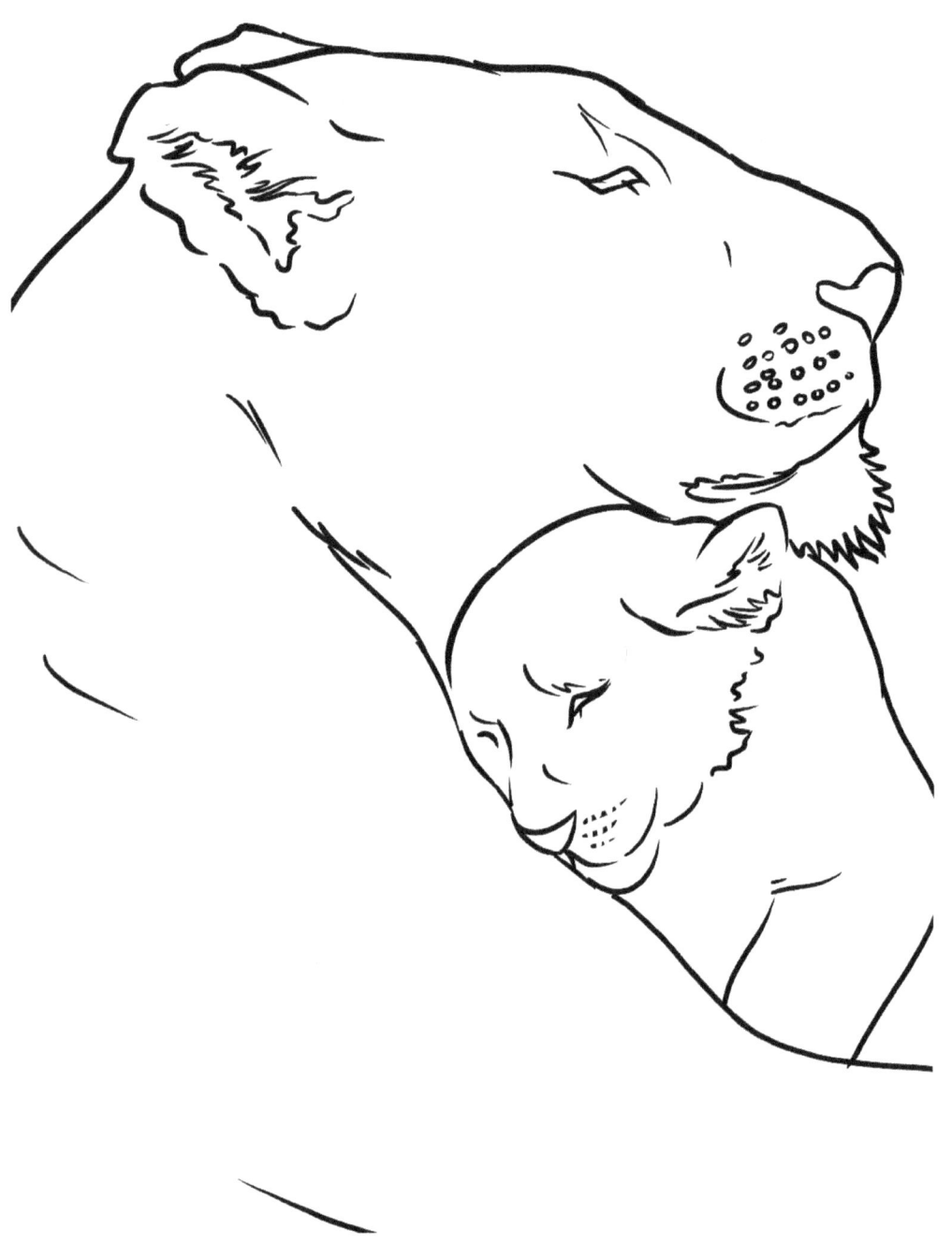

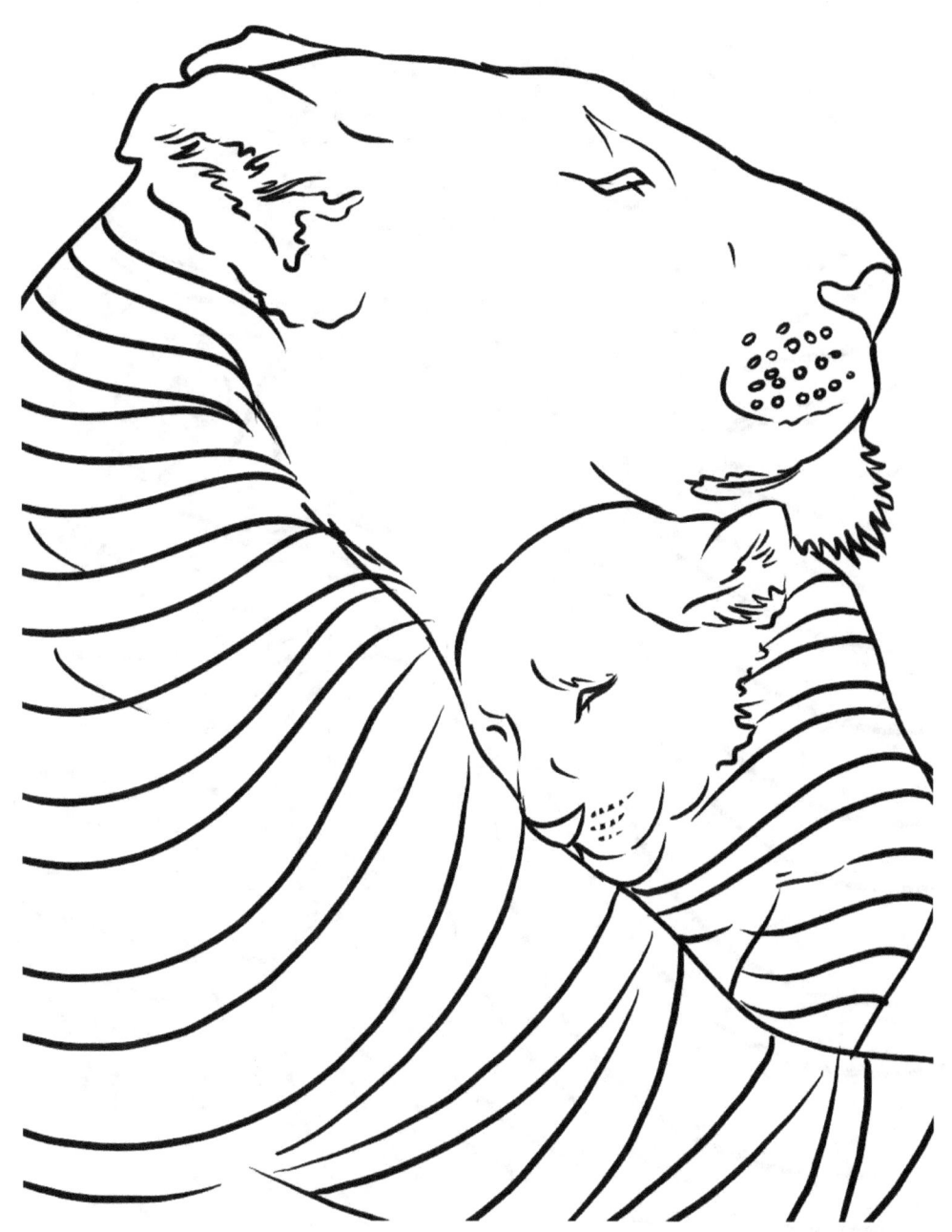

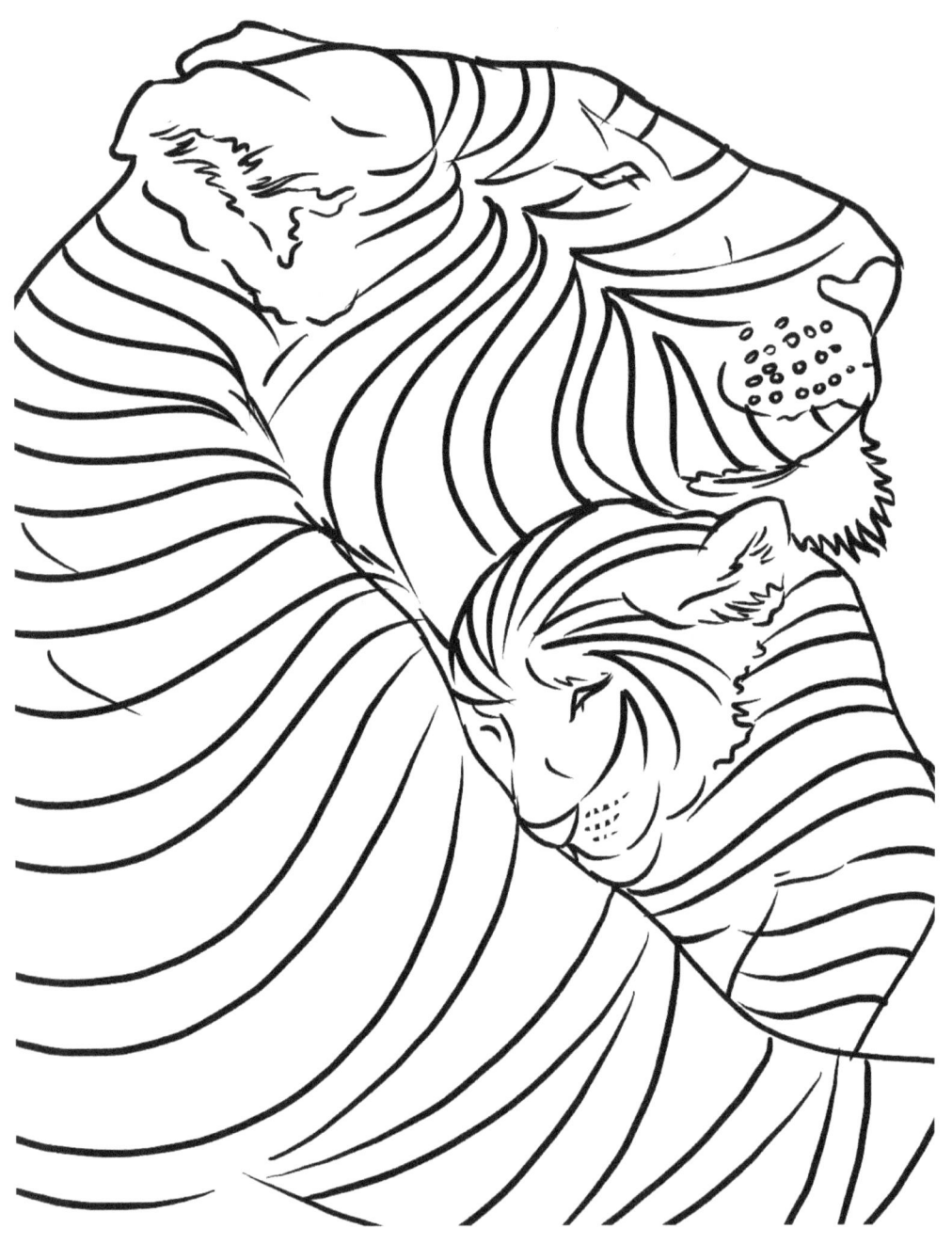

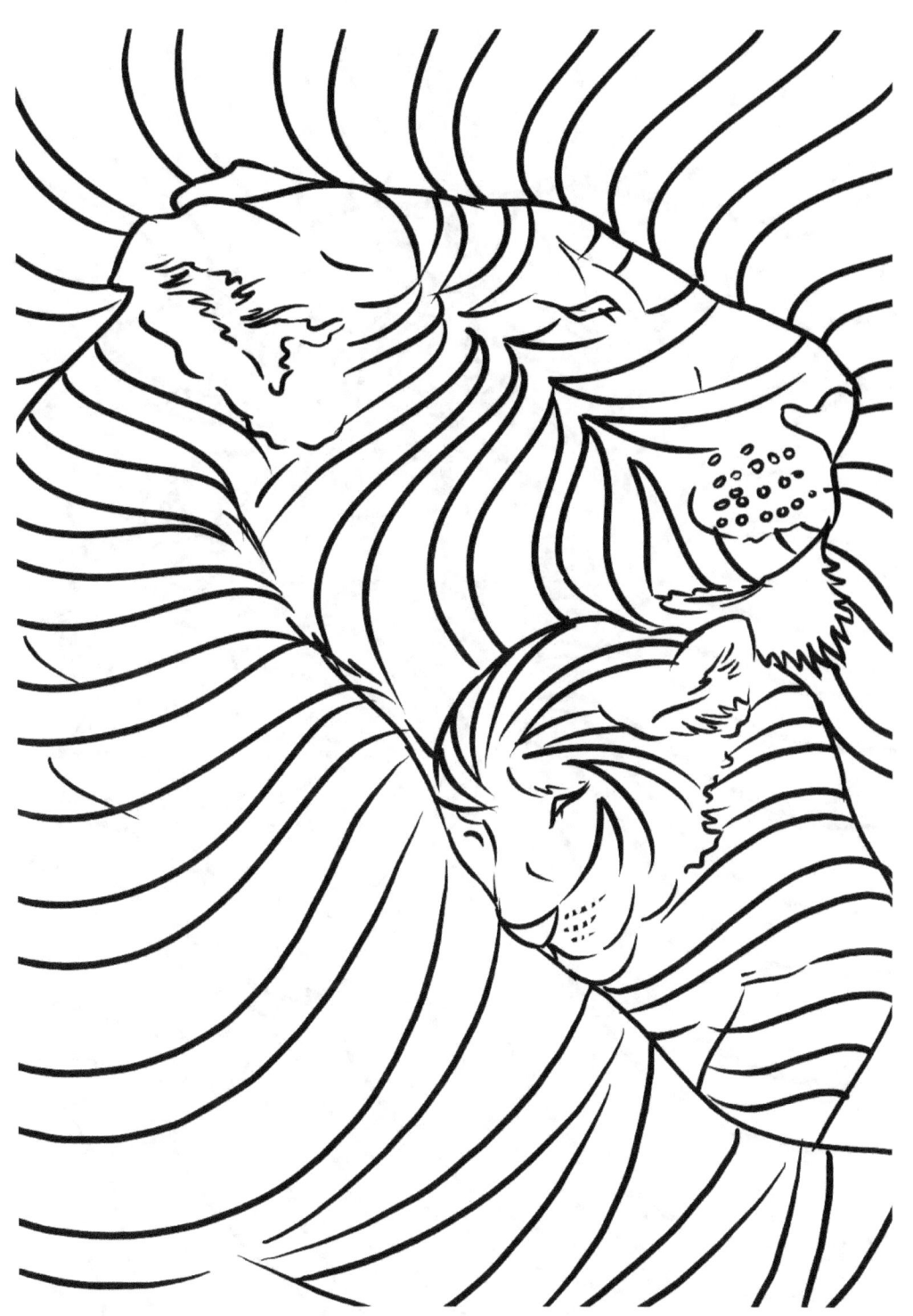

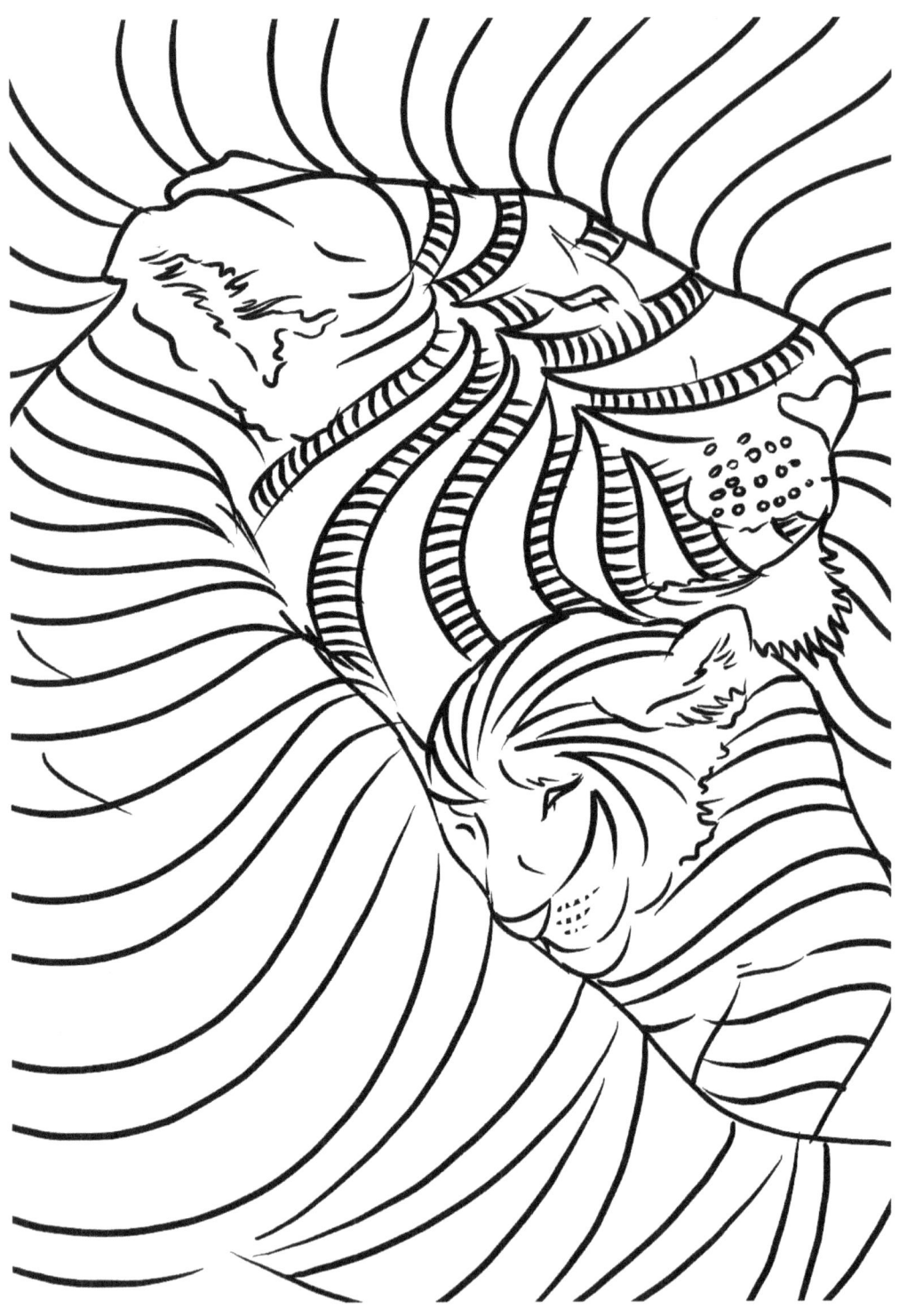

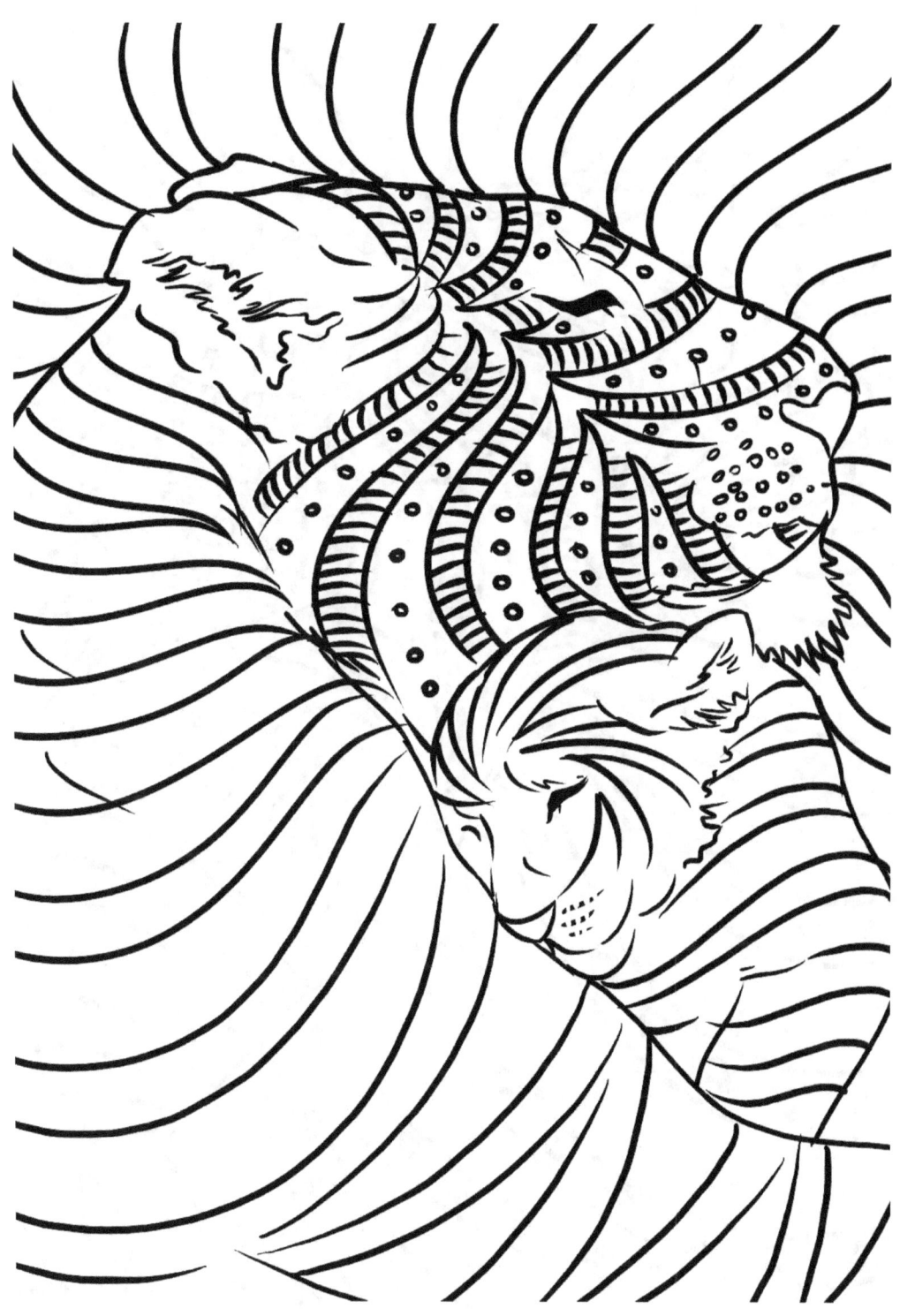

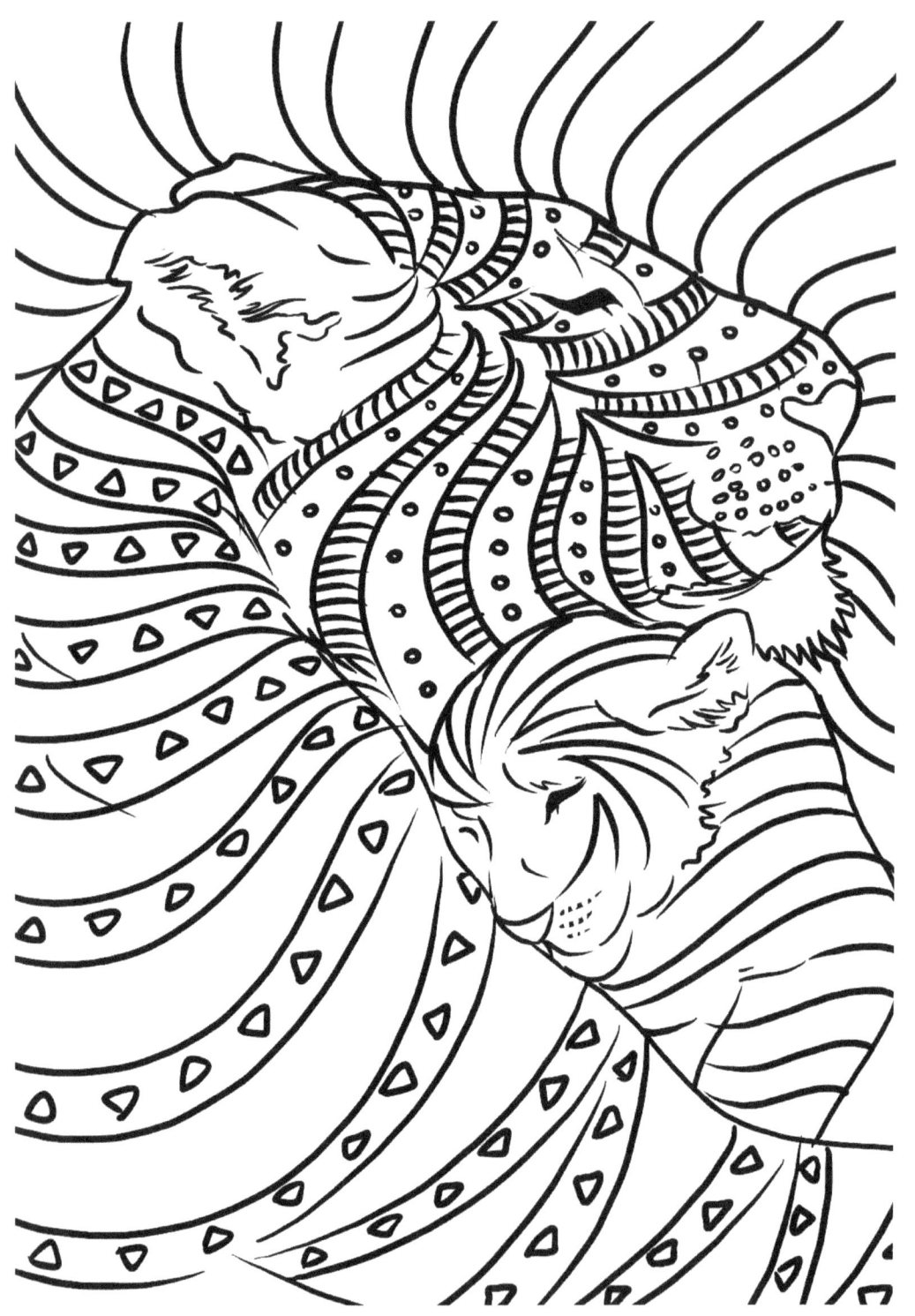

Now with these next three images you can see that the intricacies and patterns are really starting to show. This is when you need to take the skills that you learned from all those patterns at the beginning of this book and really put them to use. As you see with the line work and the repetition in shapes and design, this is exactly what you were practicing for. Don't be discouraged and keep up the good work.

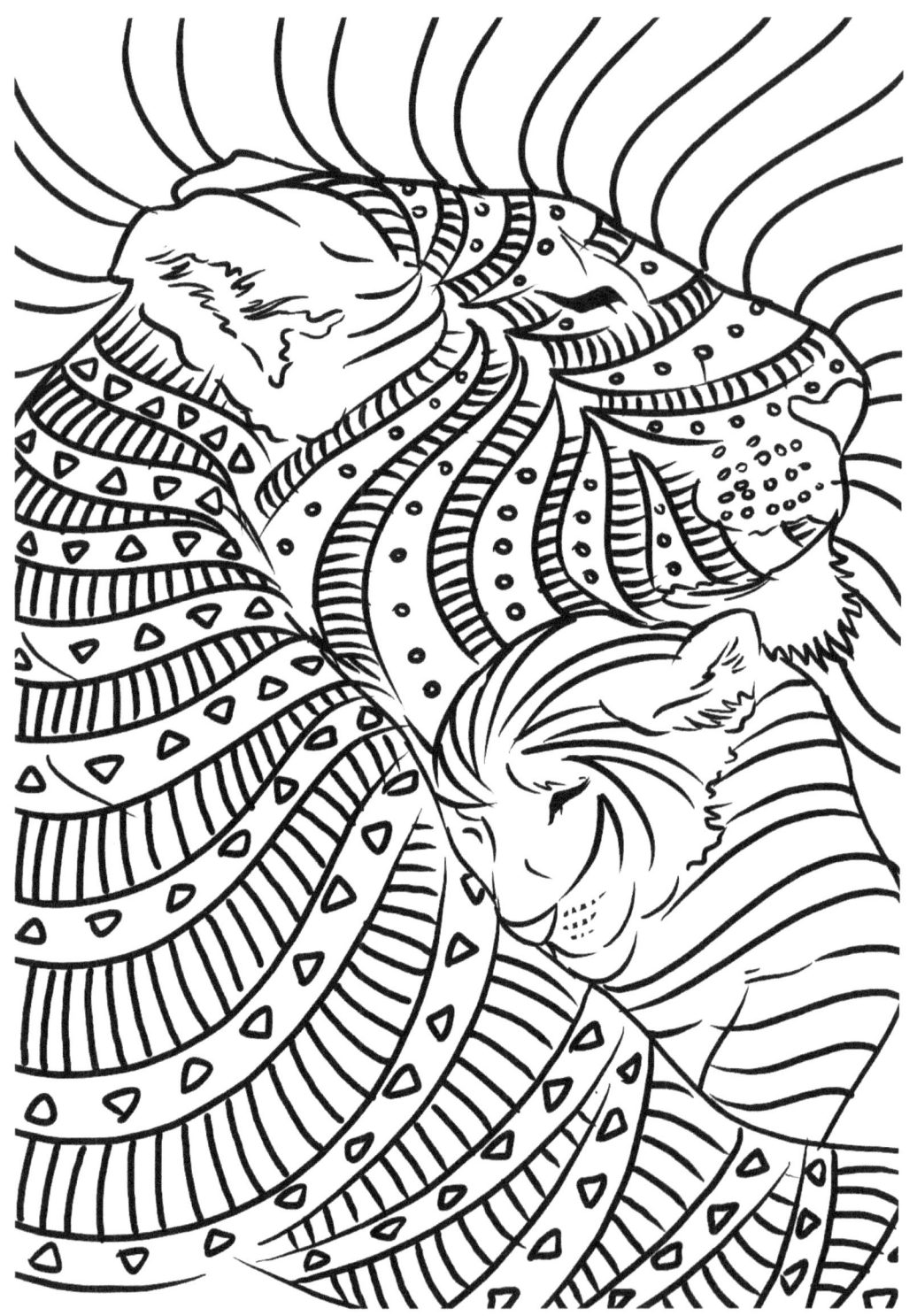

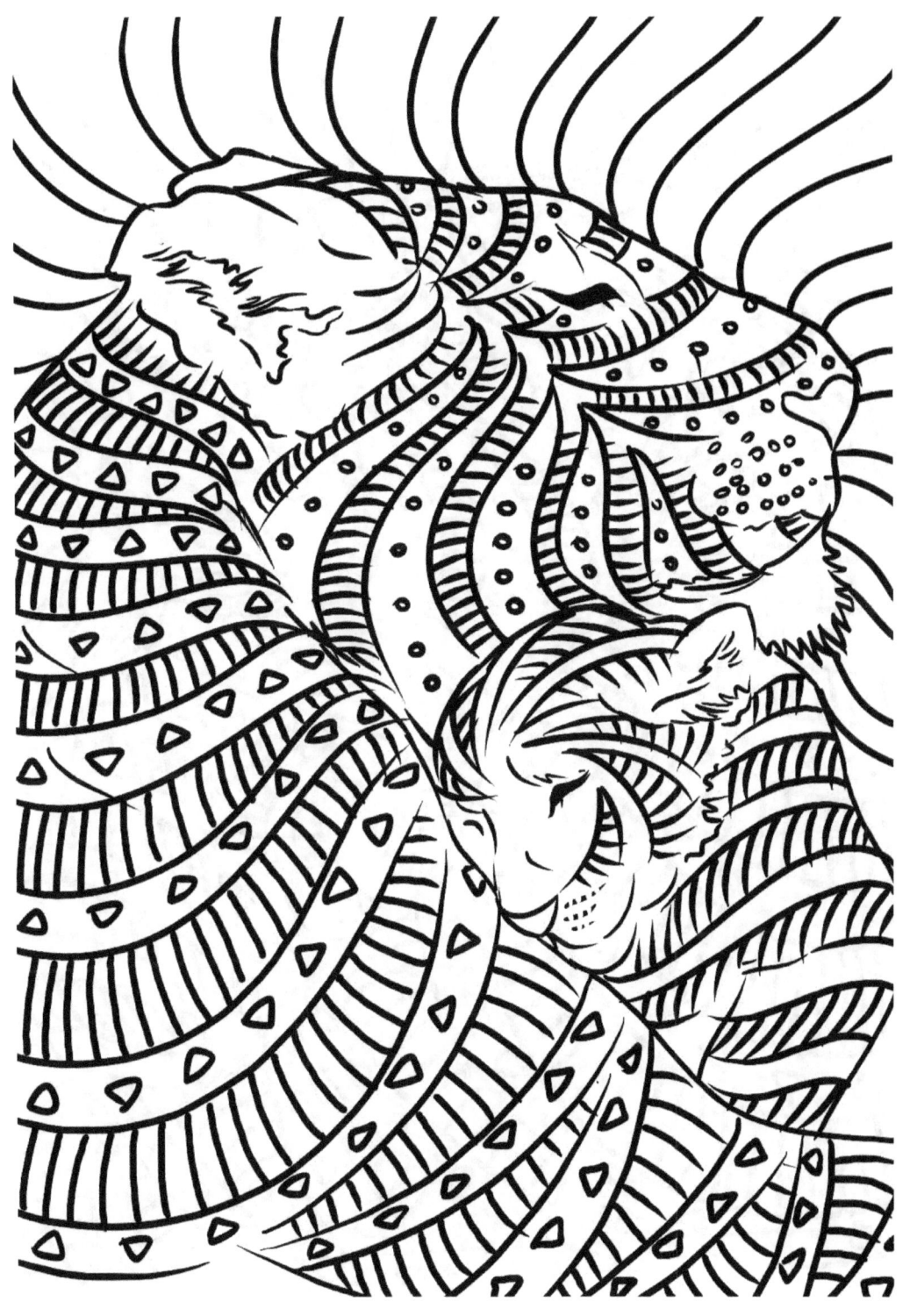

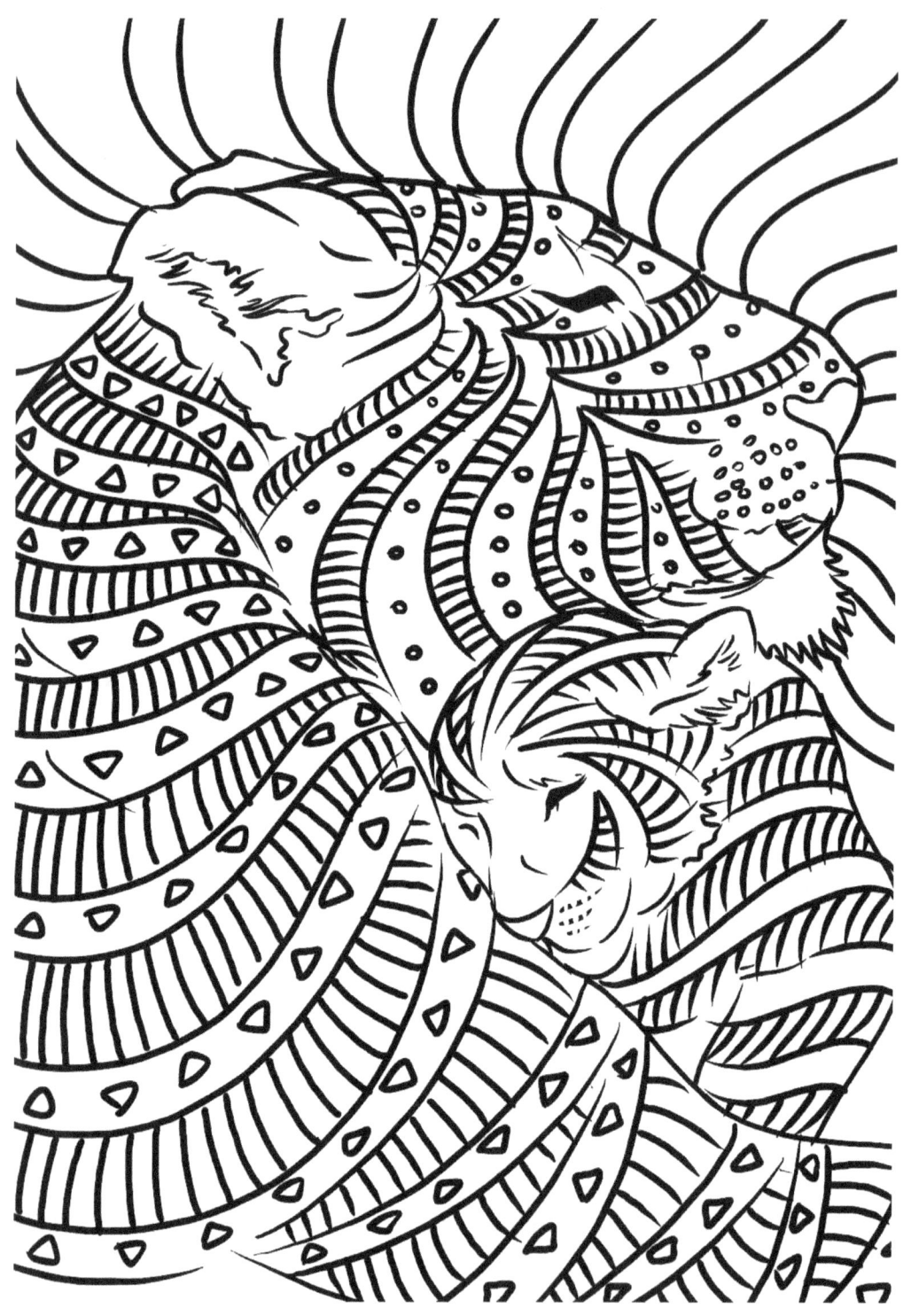

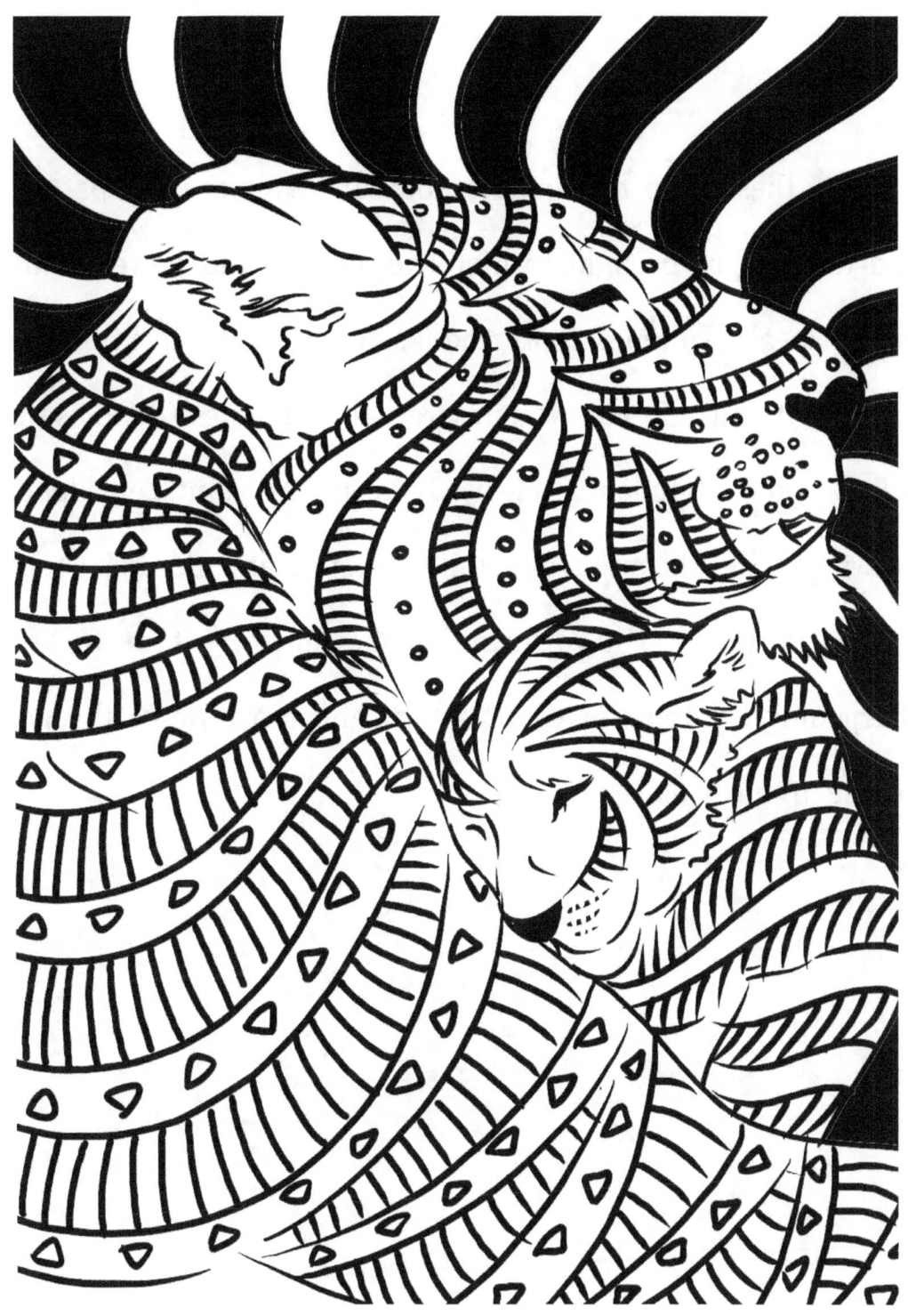

In these final two images you can really see the patterns and the designs brought to life. The ferocity and power in this image speaks volumes more thanks to the patterns utilized in bringing it to fruition. As you progress through these doodles that will become abundantly clear. Patterns in your Zen doodle drawings will add miles and miles of style and flourish to the images. Now that you've finished this image it's time to keep sharpening the tools in your tool kit and move on to the next doodle in this book.

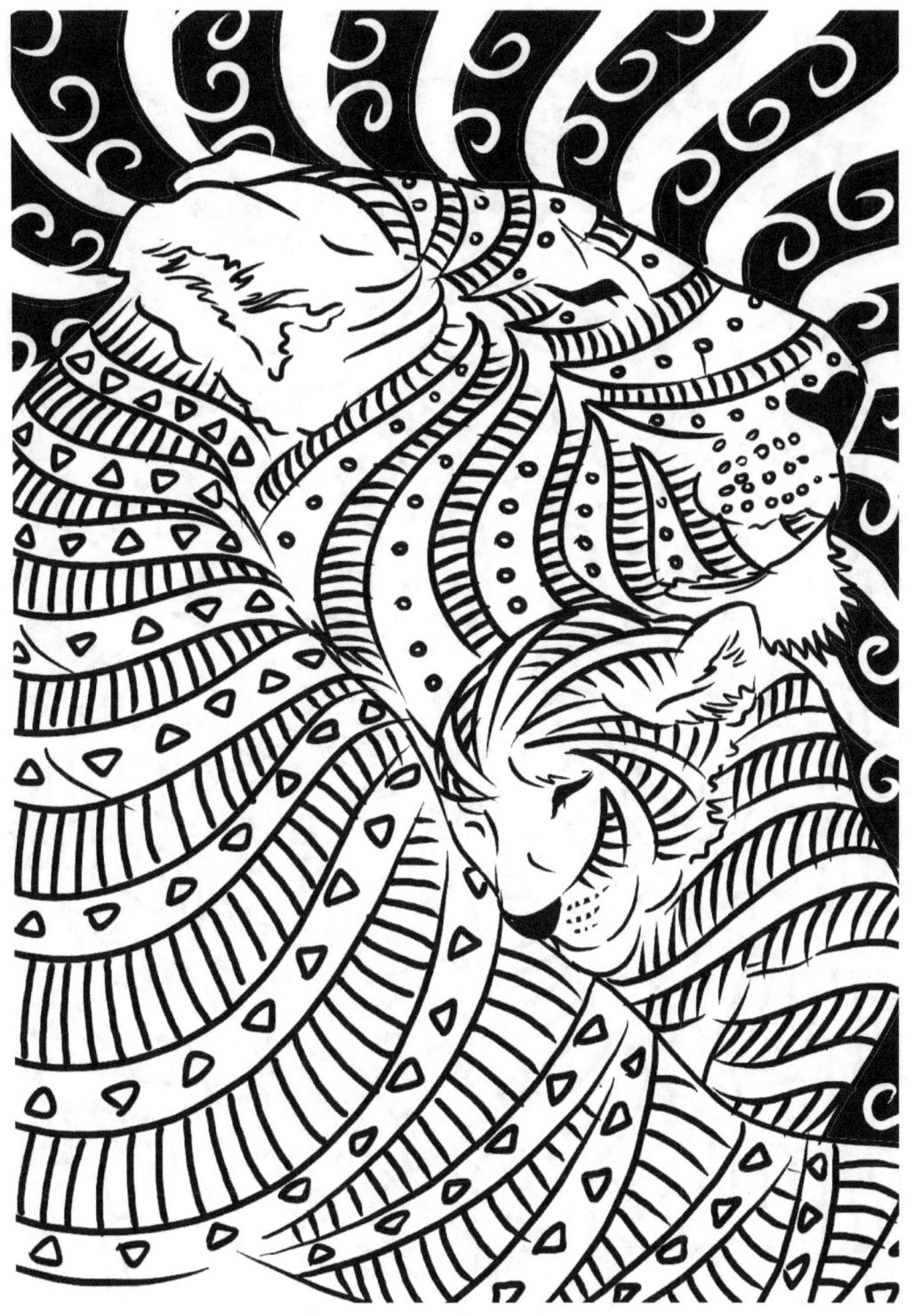

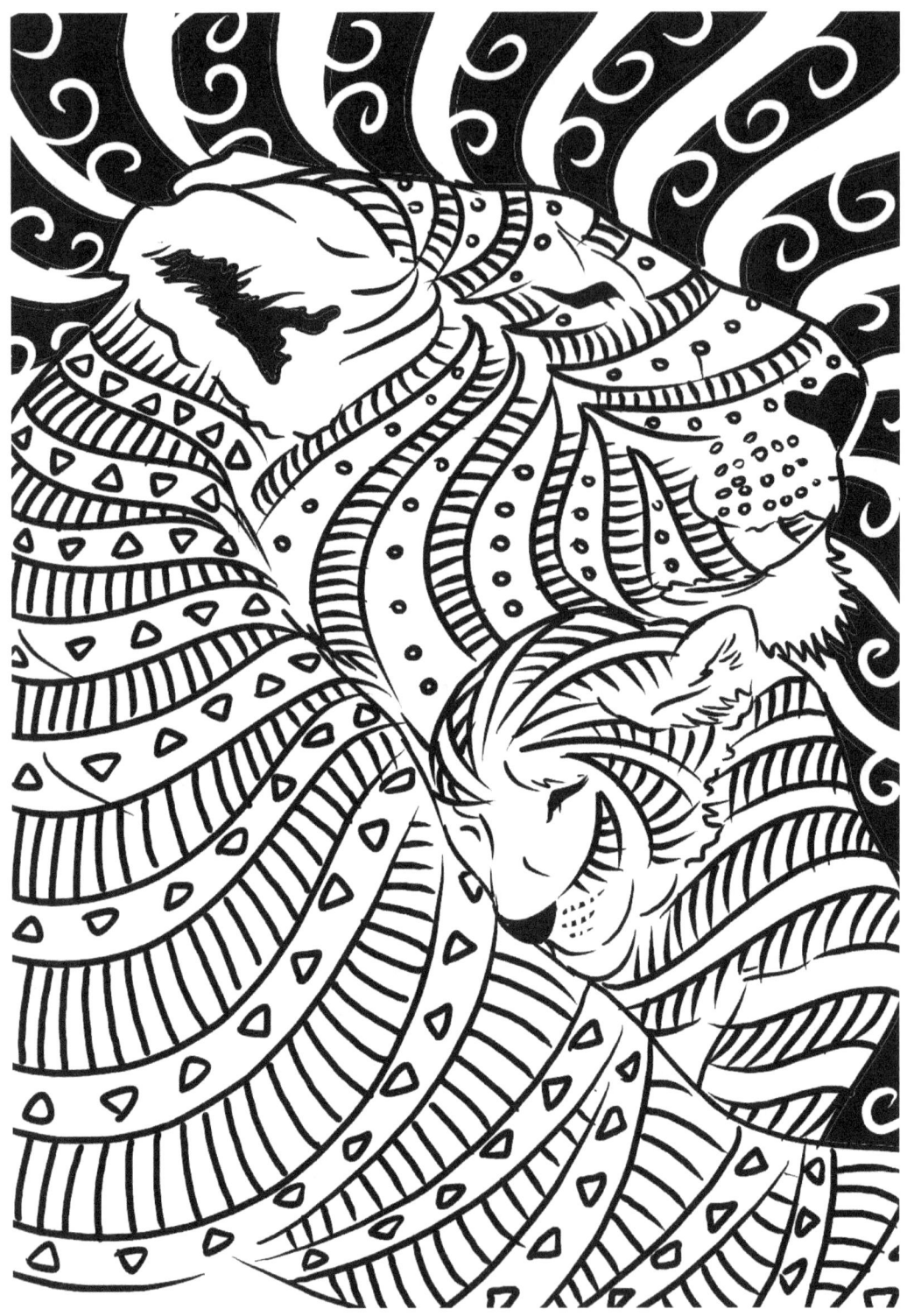

Doodle 2 – Eagle

Just as the last one began so does this one. The simple line work that lays down the ground work for everything else to come. To start off this eagle you'll be using softer lines and not as many hard edges. Yet by the last image you can see there's already shading coming in to play, safe to assume that when shading gets brought up, there will be some tougher moves up ahead as well on the horizon. Looking down to the next three images you can see that line work starts to build up and get more fantastical. Push through that and again remember to use what you've learned in this book as of yet and continue to the next set of images.

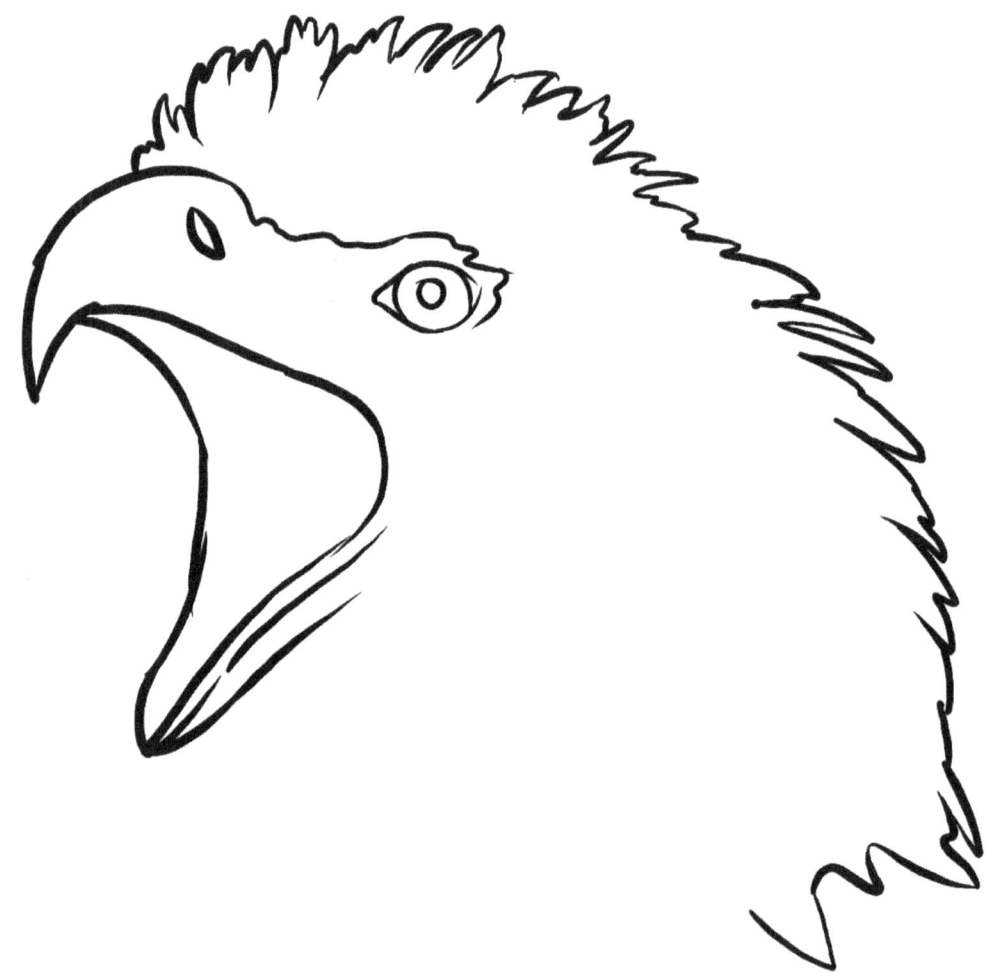

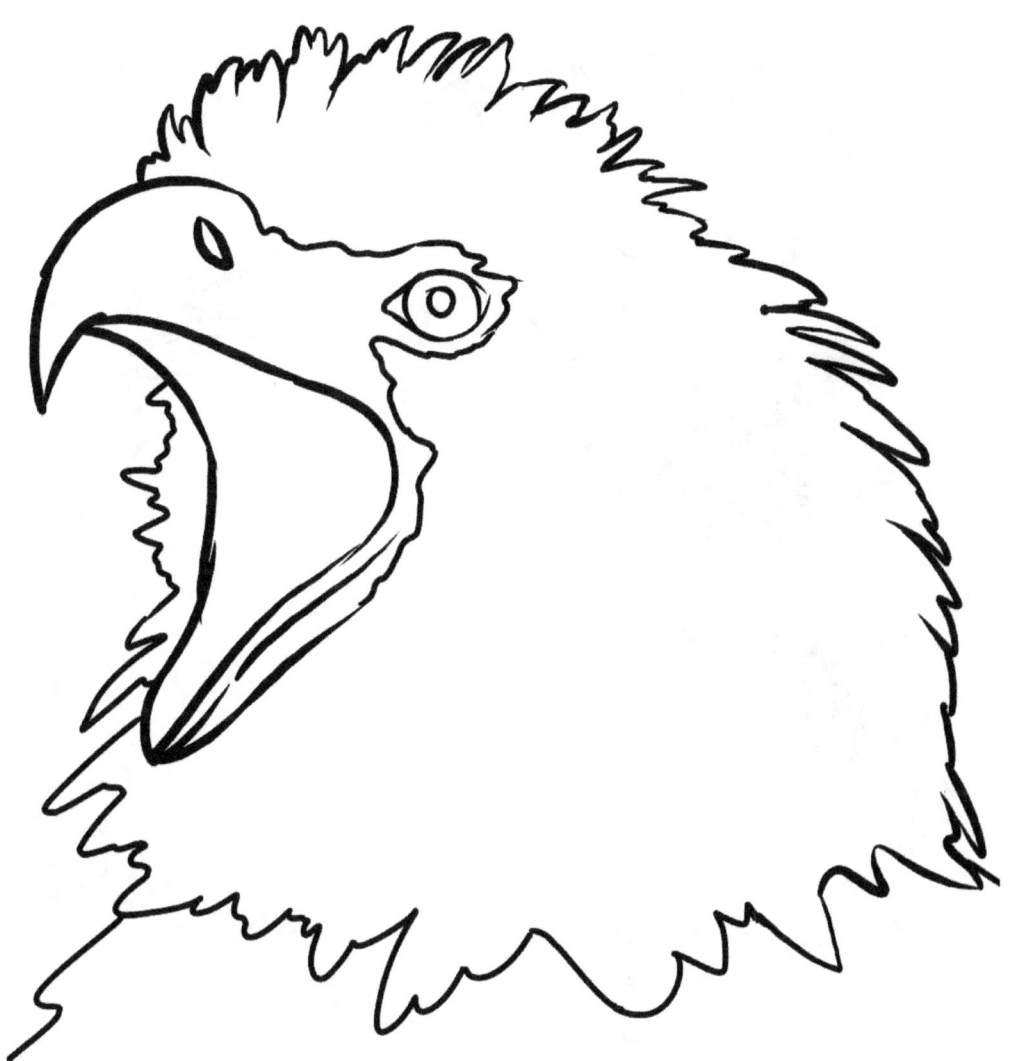

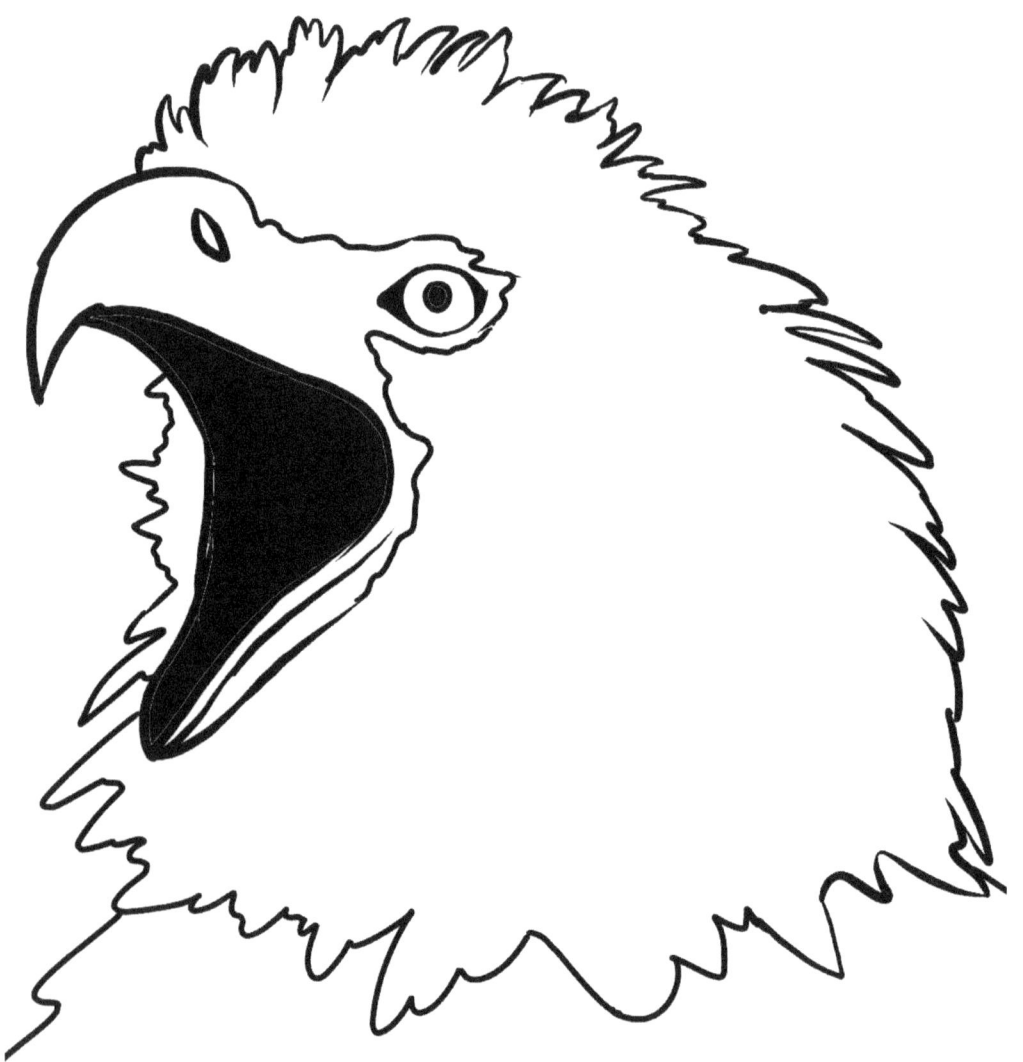

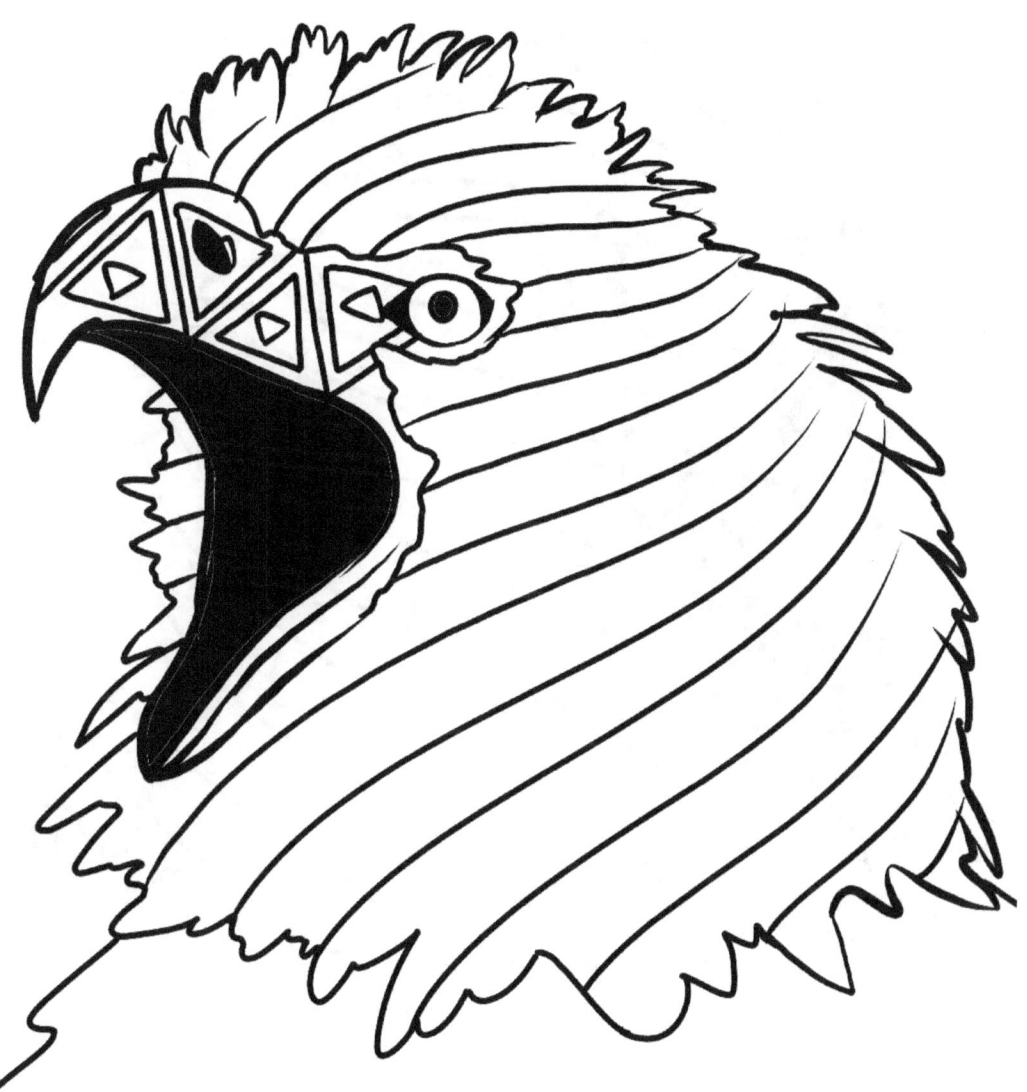

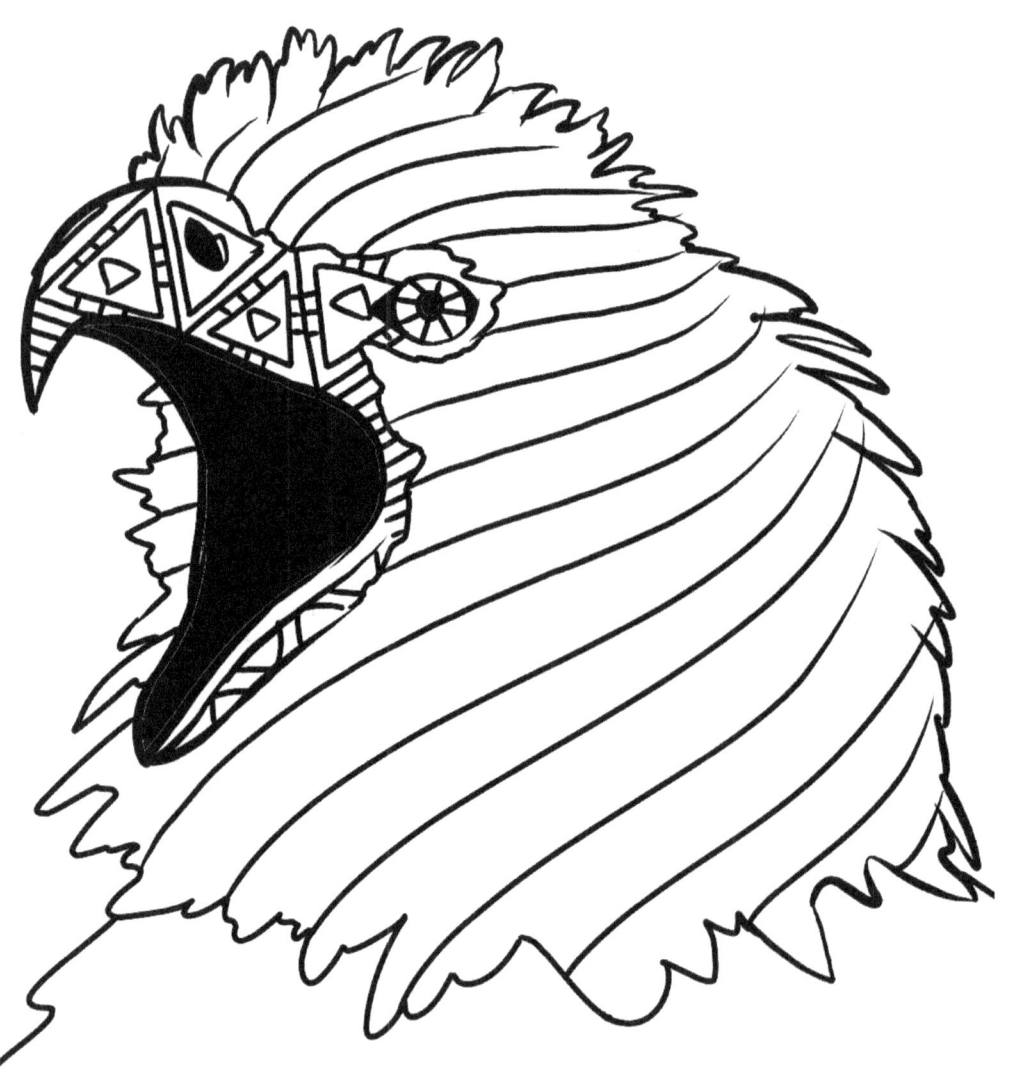

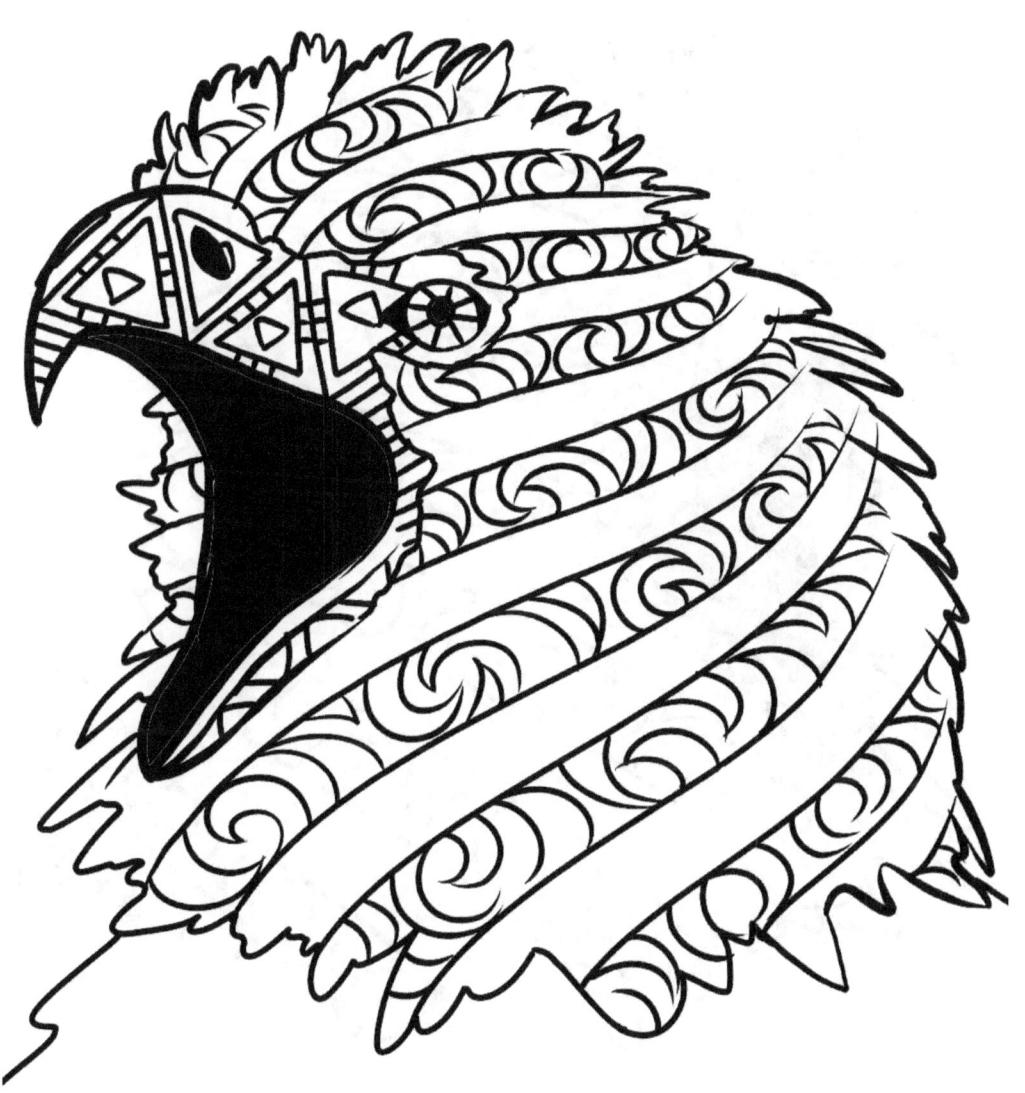

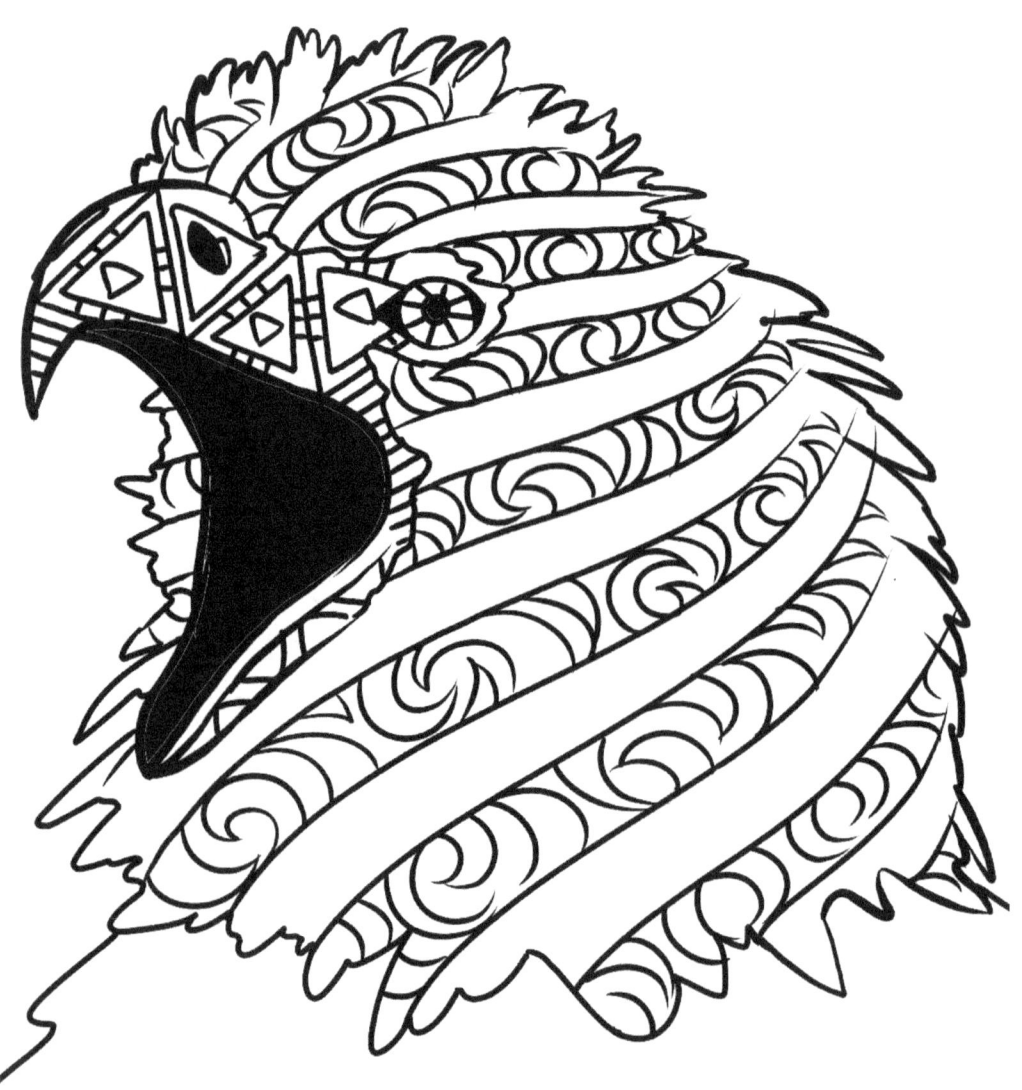

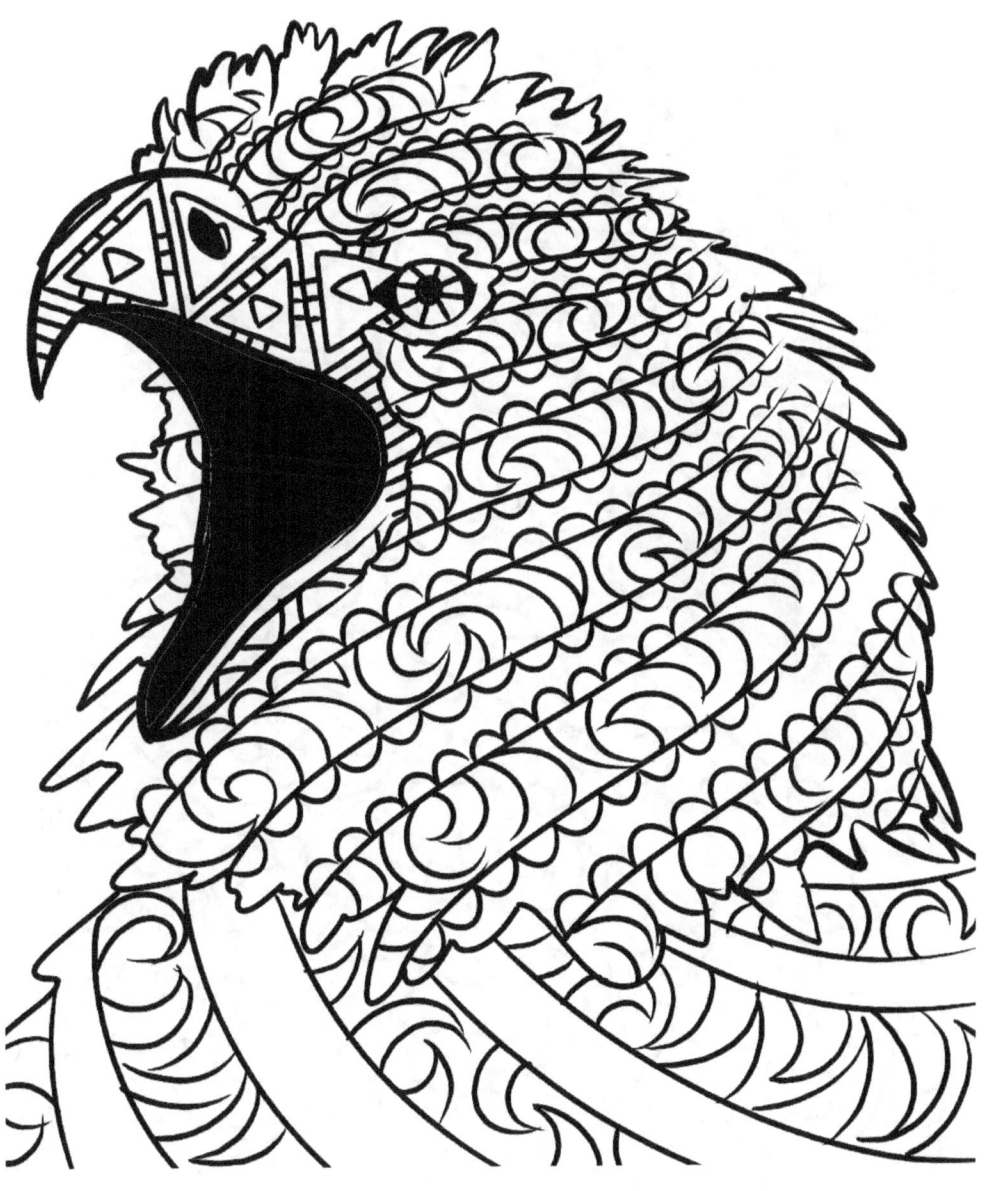

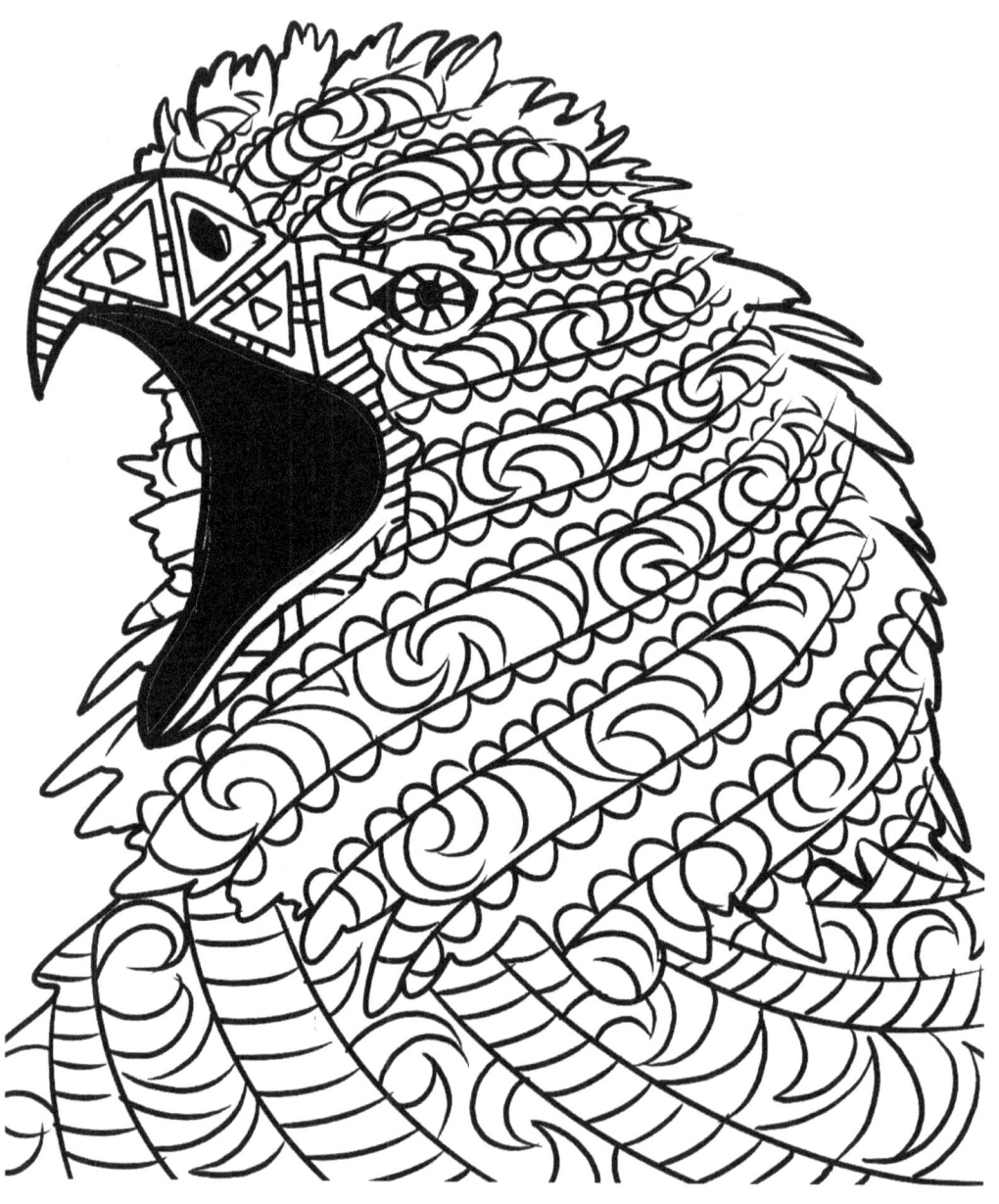

Now we take it up quite a few notches as the line work gets way more elaborate and becomes a full-fledged and very self-involved pattern. The trick here is to start one line at a time with extra focus and to not let the surrounding areas distract you as you progress through the pattern. The biggest mistake you could make at this juncture is trying to hurry. You'll also notice that in these images above we start really adding the flavor to the wing area. That moves forward in the next two images when we add flowers to the background. These fill the background and add a seriously polished and finished look to the image. Something it might not have had without the background. Not all doodles need backgrounds, but this one definitely benefits. Keep that in mind as you move on to the next doodle in this comprehensive guide nook.

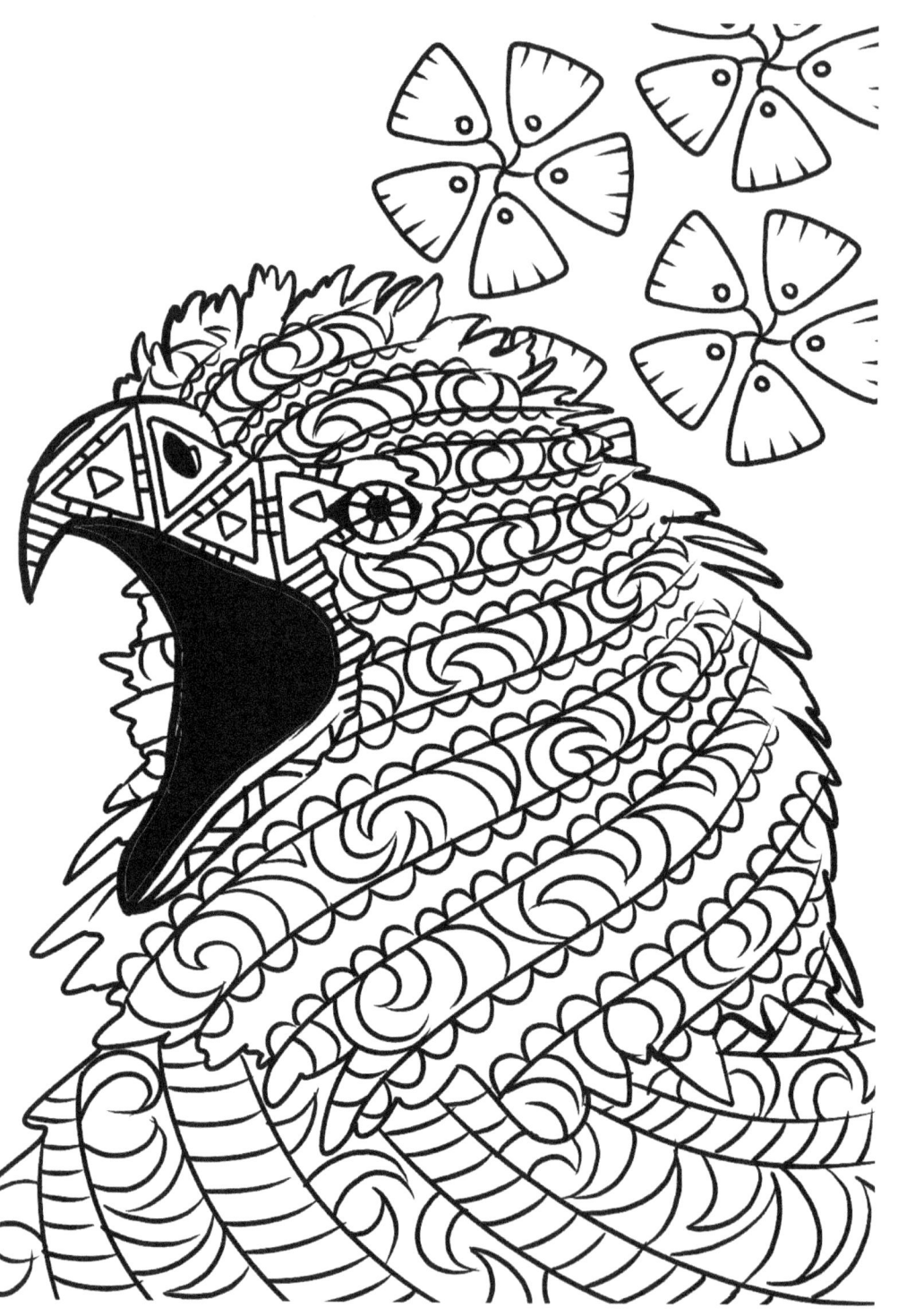

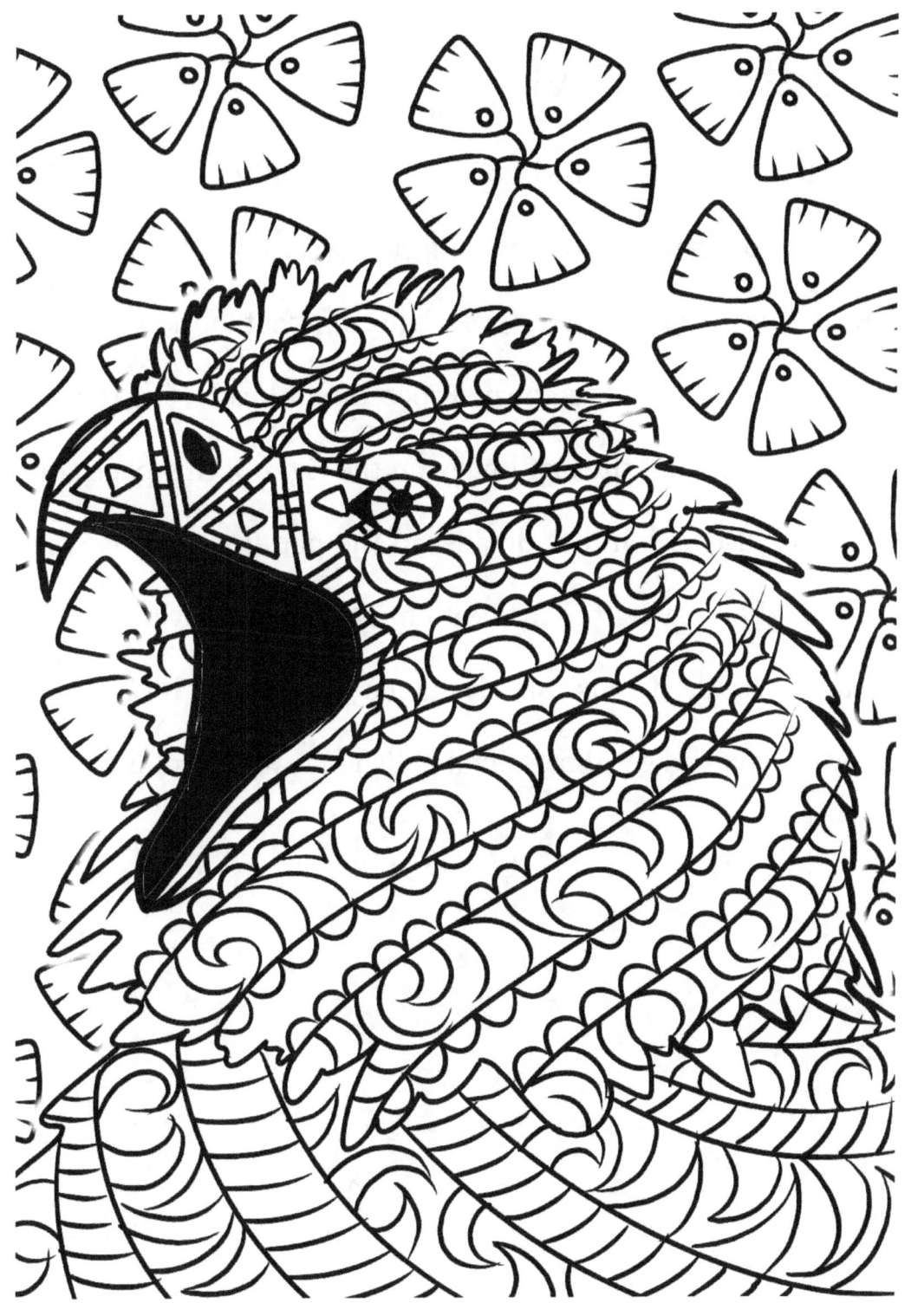

Doodle 3 – Owl

Here we have an owl doodle starting off with the nice line work. As you can see we have angrier eyes, unless you wish to change them yourself! However ignoring that option, proceed with the drawing as is shown. Proceeding ahead with the next steps you'll see that the last image on the right of this page starts with the intricacies in the detail and the pattern. Here is where you should be paying the most attention and really watching the small minuscule details. Steady hands are needed here, so just believe in you and get those small polished features rolling!

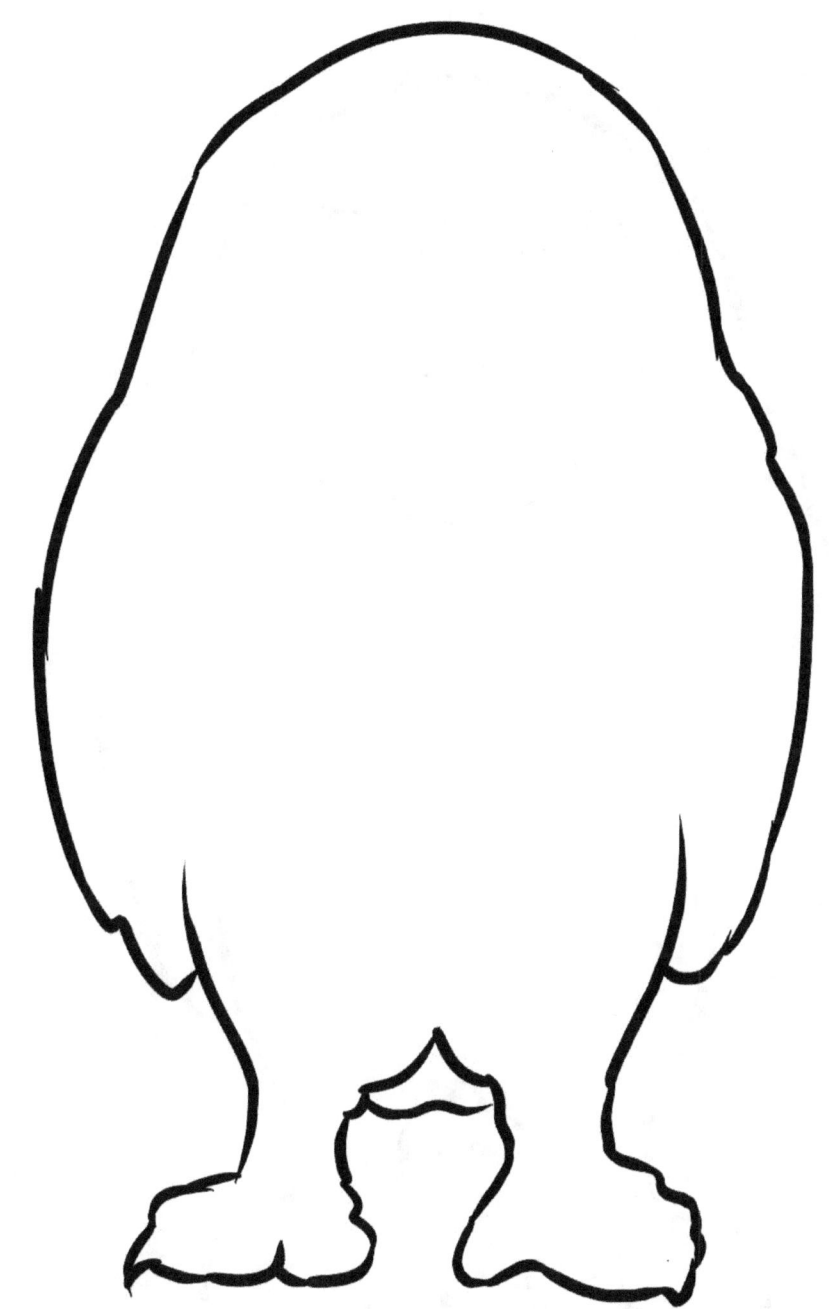

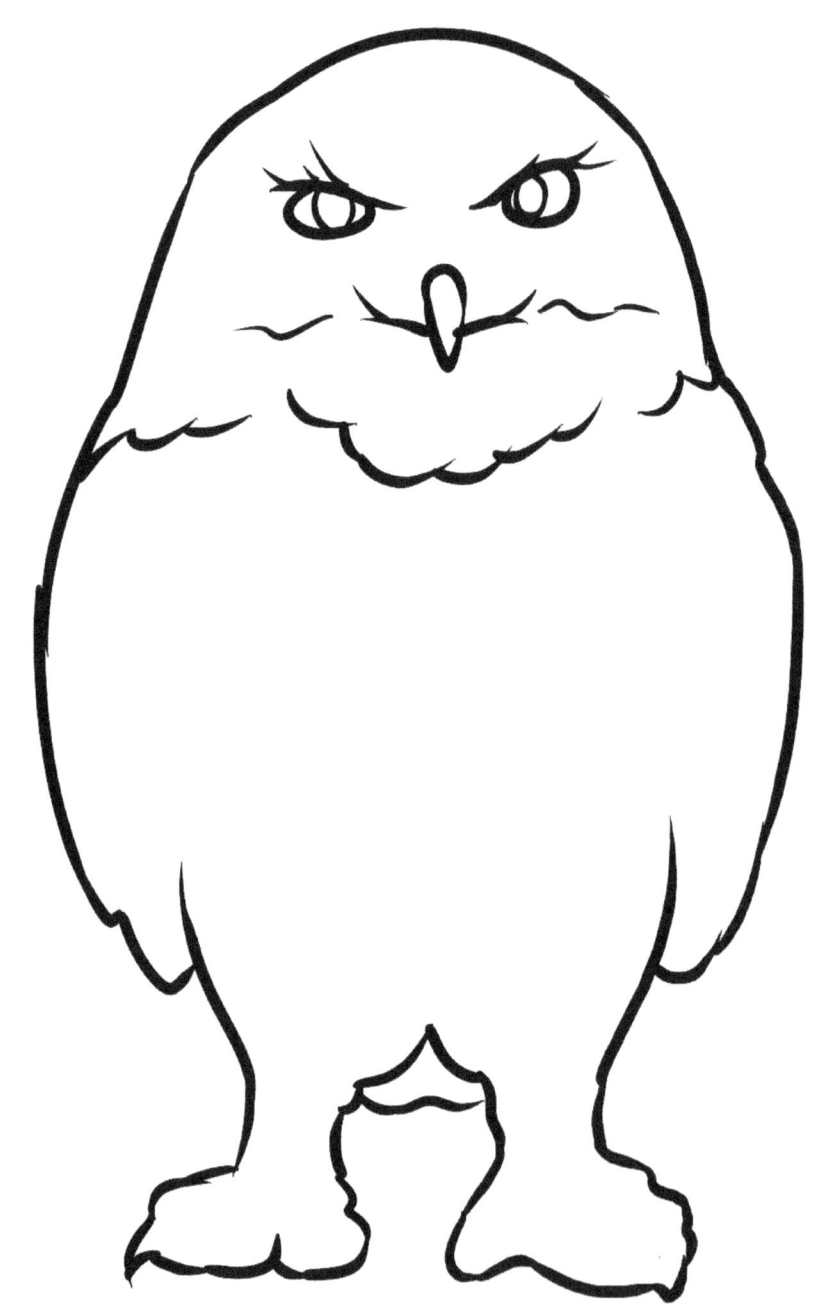

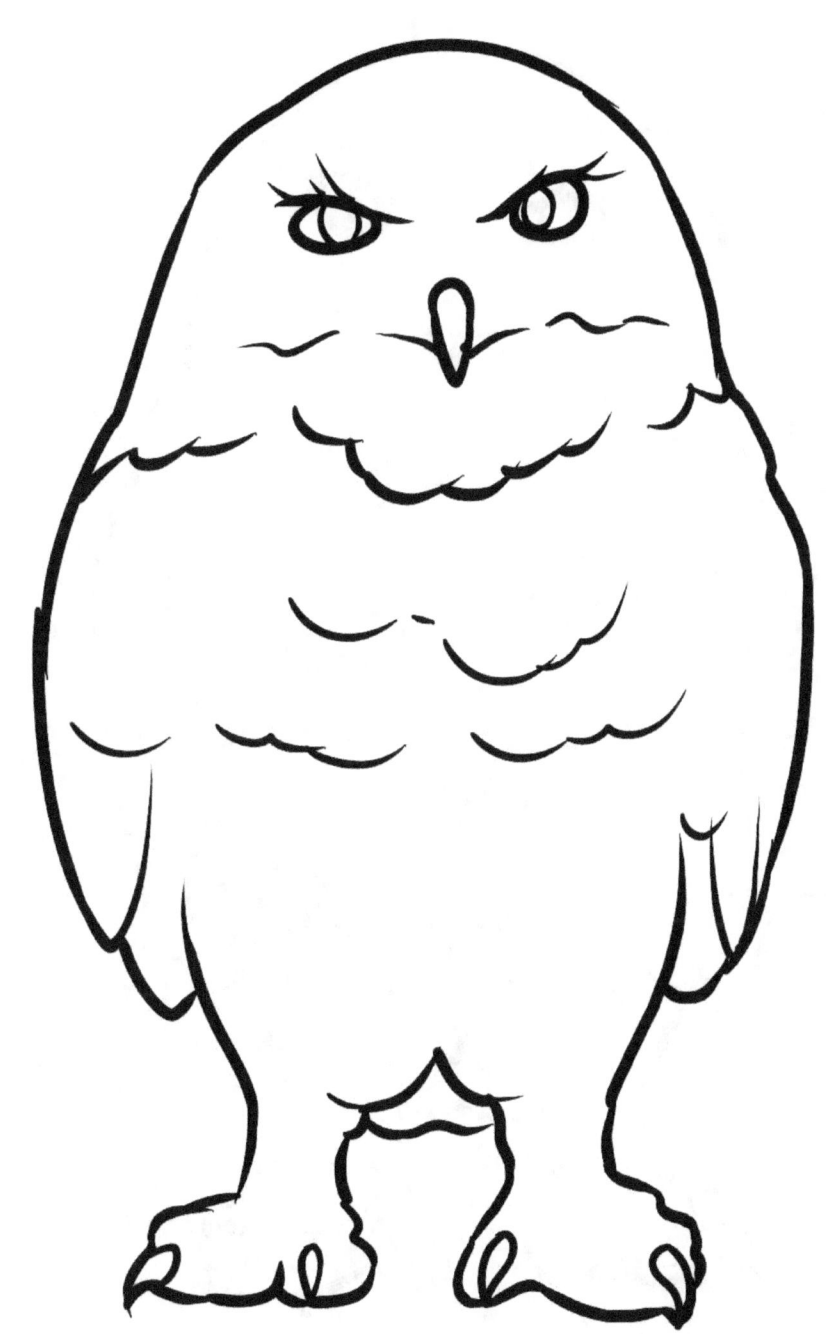

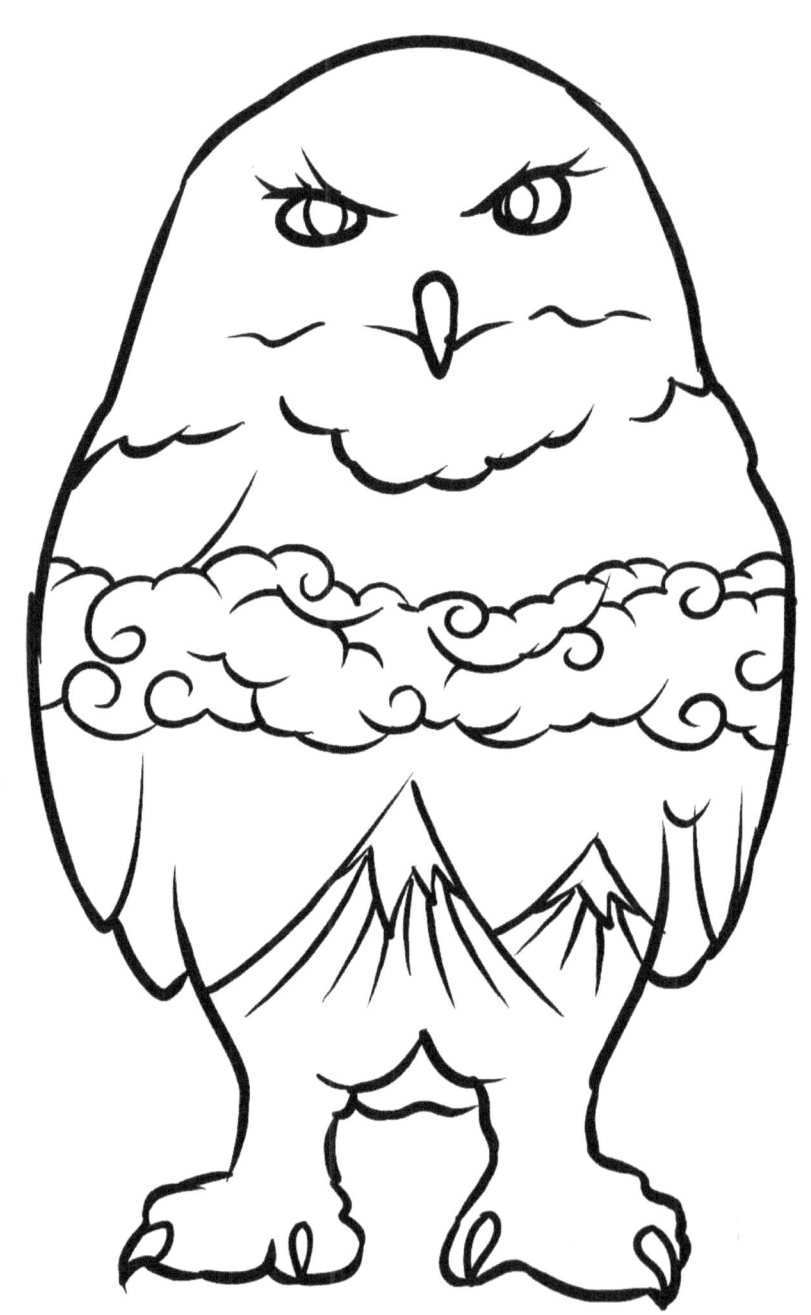

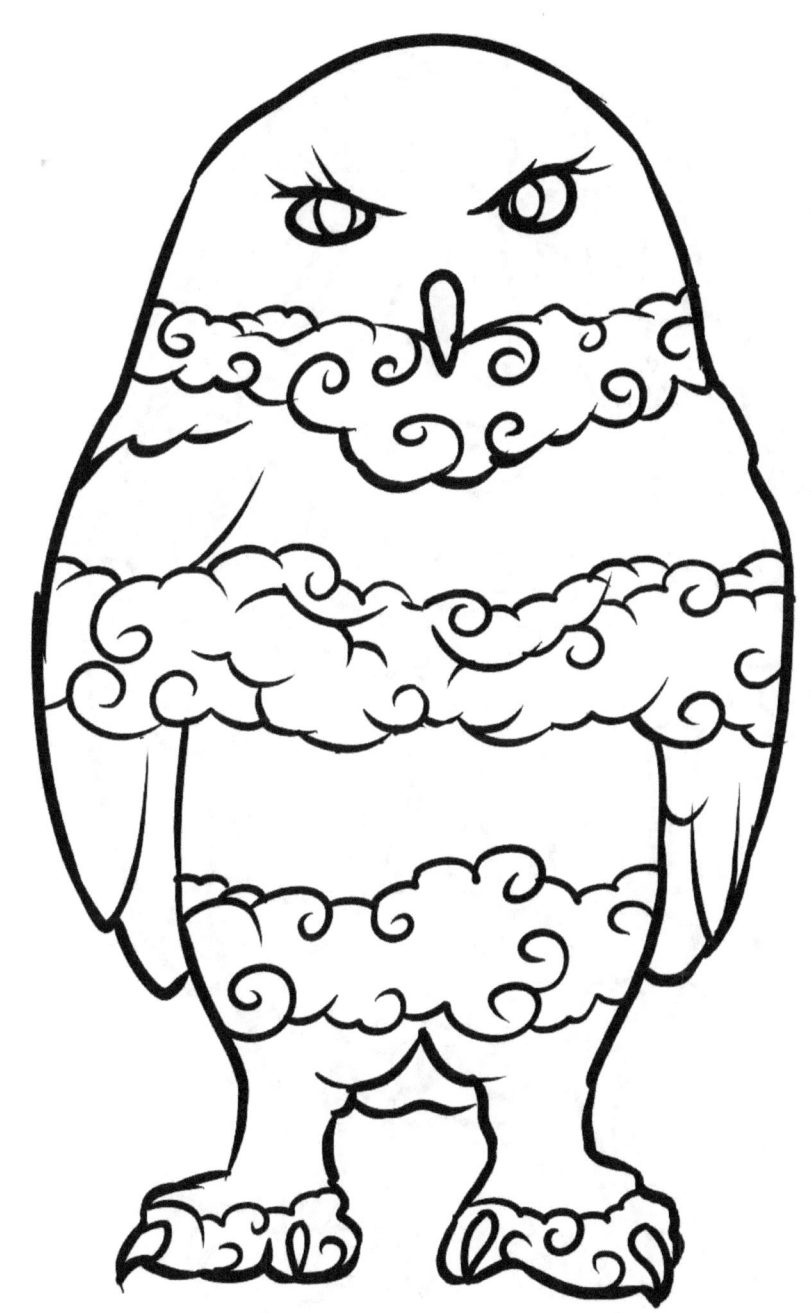

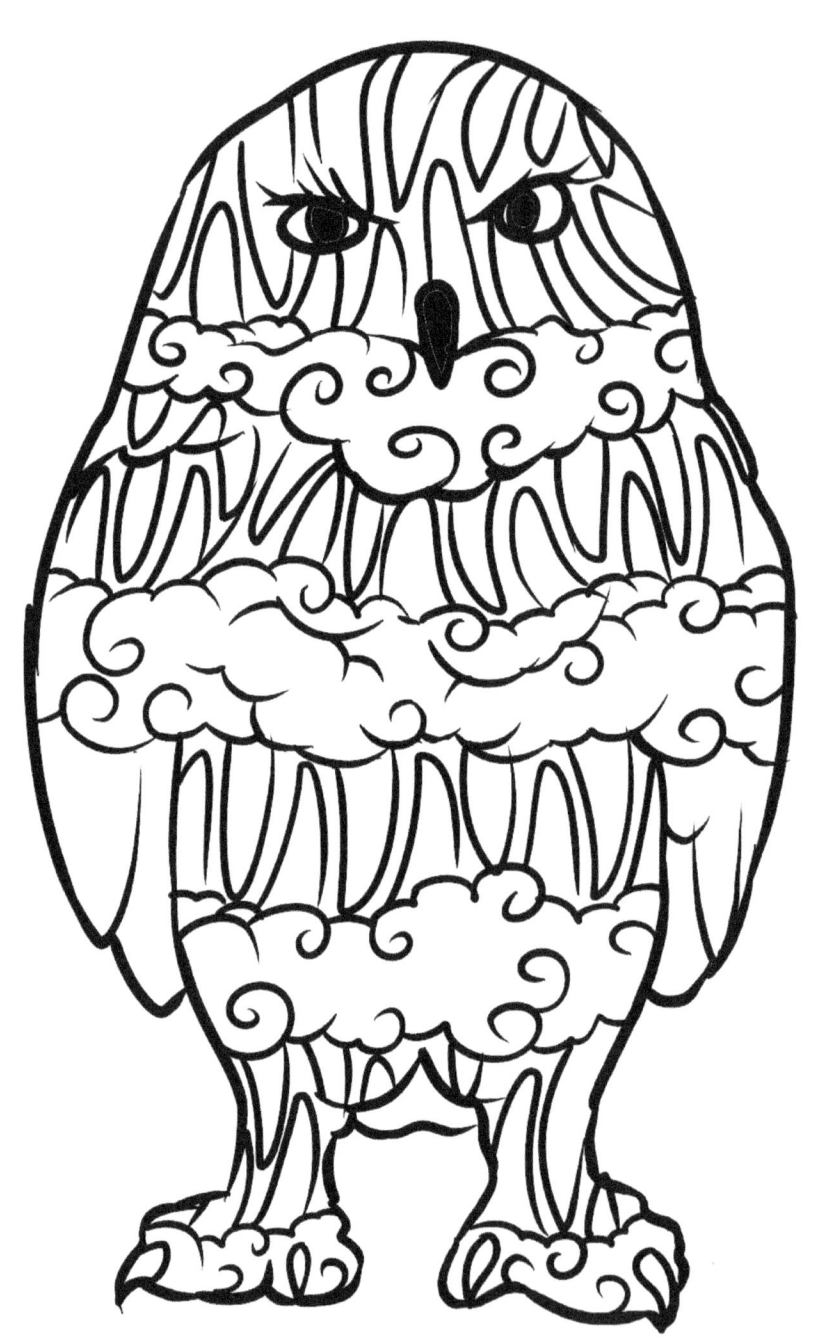

These next six images have a lot of shading work and the even finer details pertaining to what's done with the shaded in background. This is the segment where having great patience will be a much more useful tool than any rulers or protractors will be. An area of great detail that I would like to point out at this juncture is the cloud like pattern in between the layers on the owl. I think that area is both a really great design and a tricky spot. Try not to get caught up on it as you finish up this design! The next step is to get even more in depth and just dive in to the final three images extravagancies!

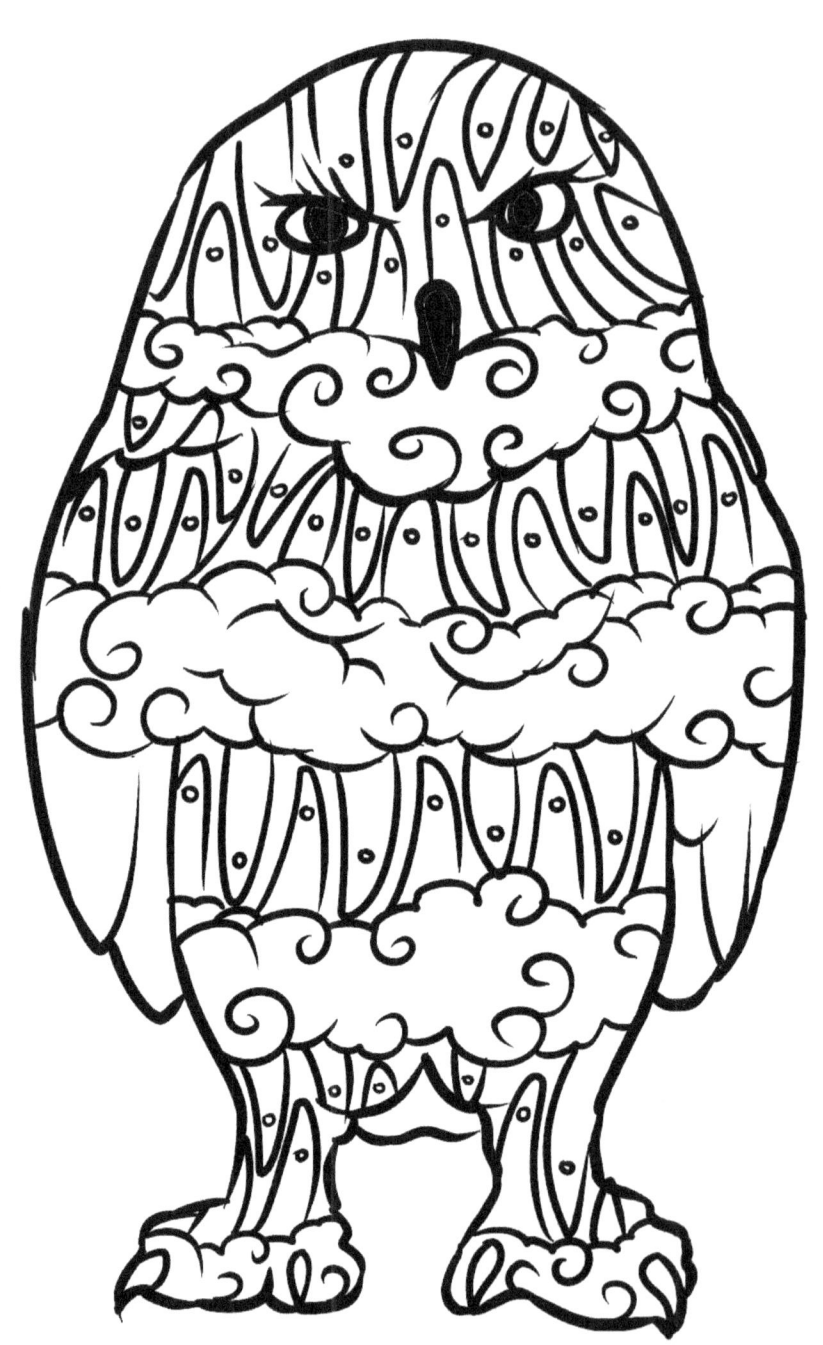

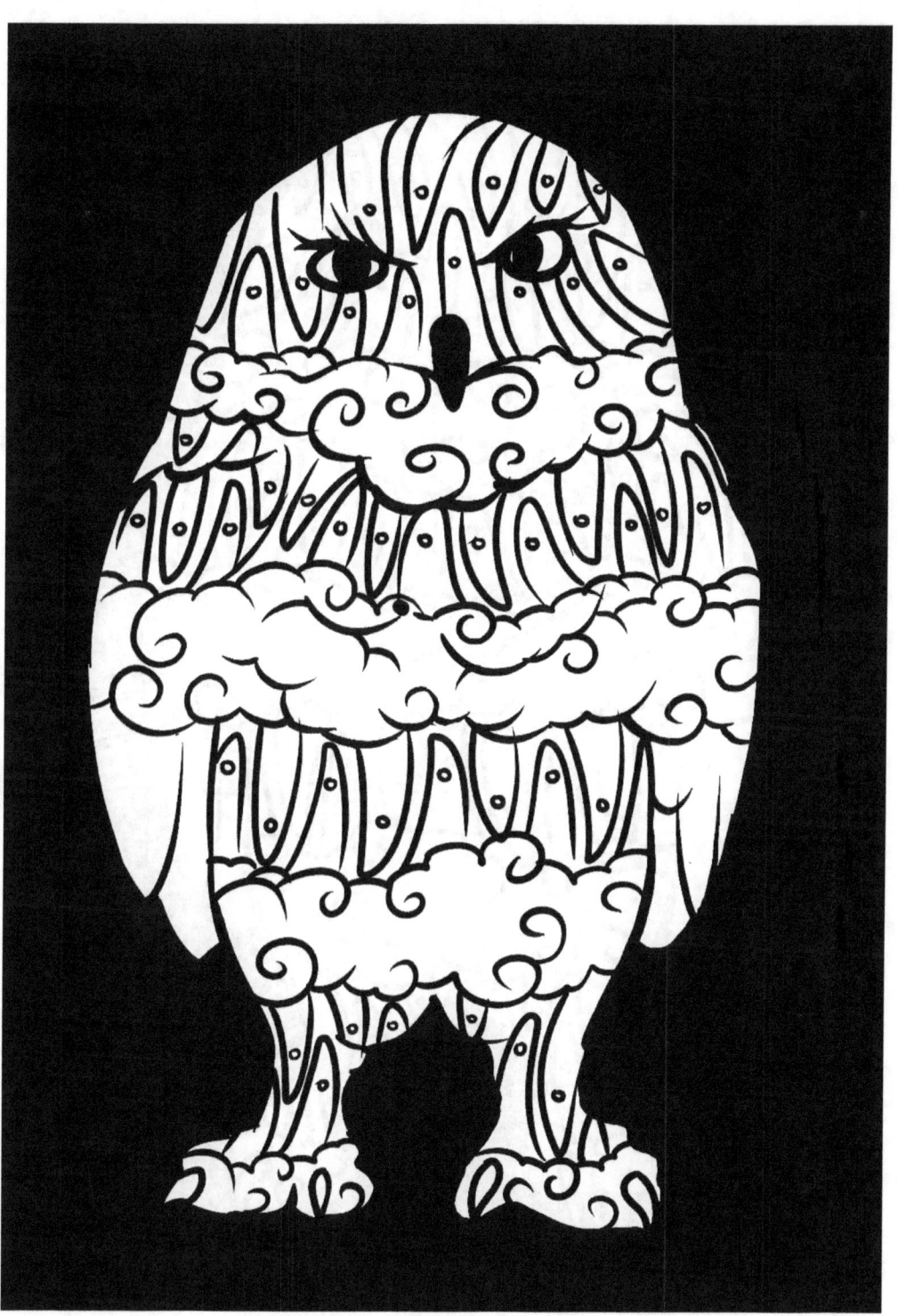

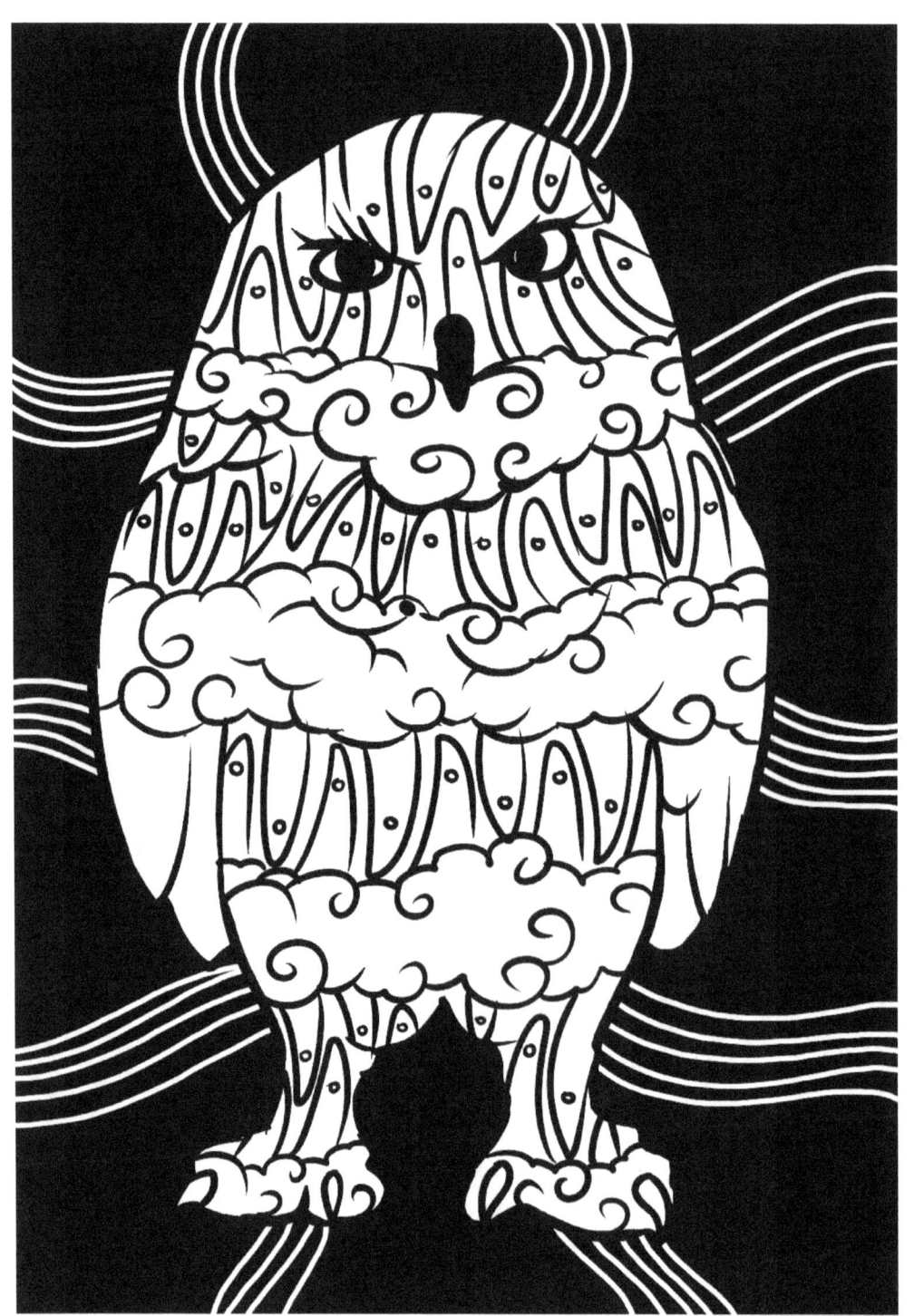

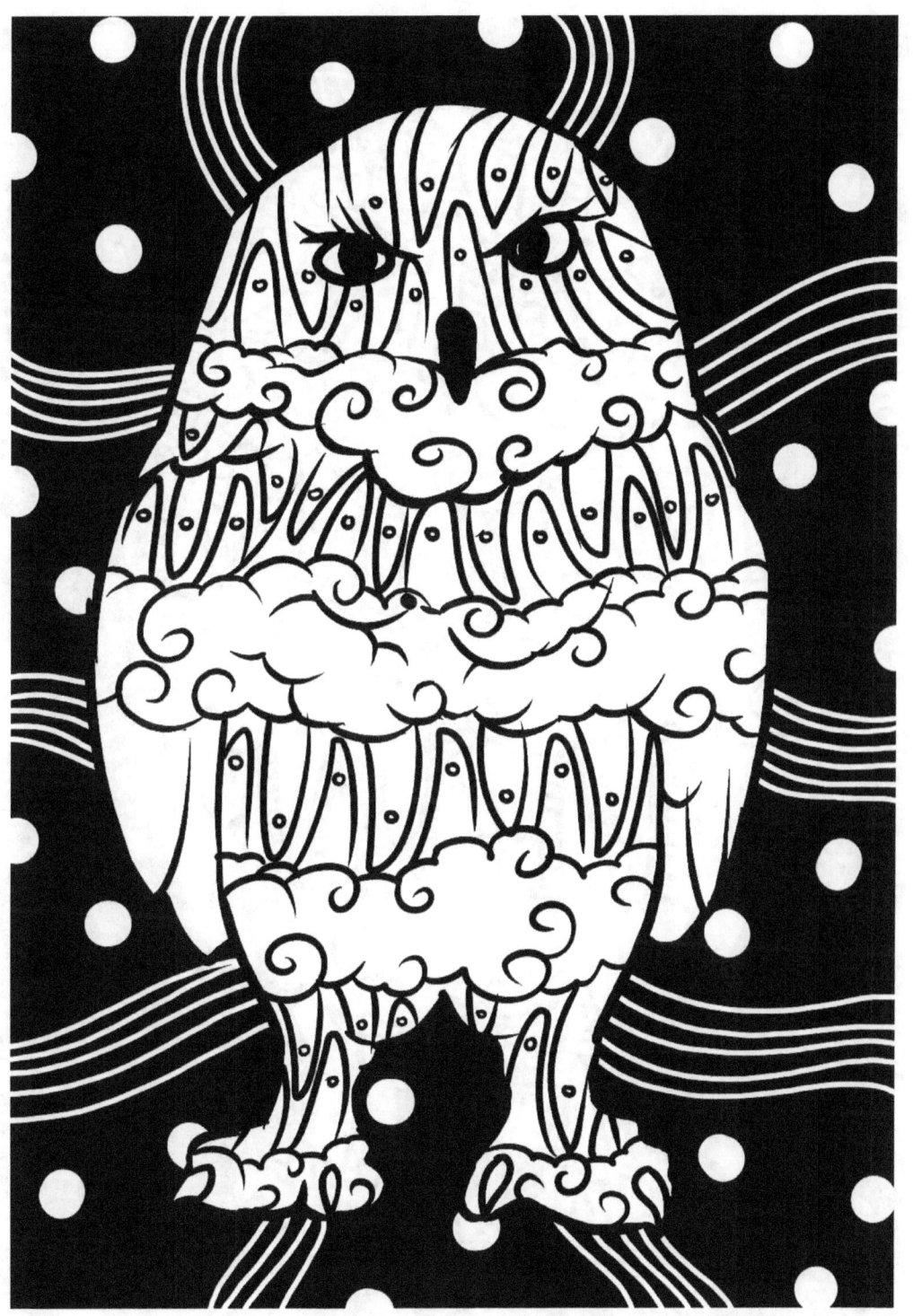

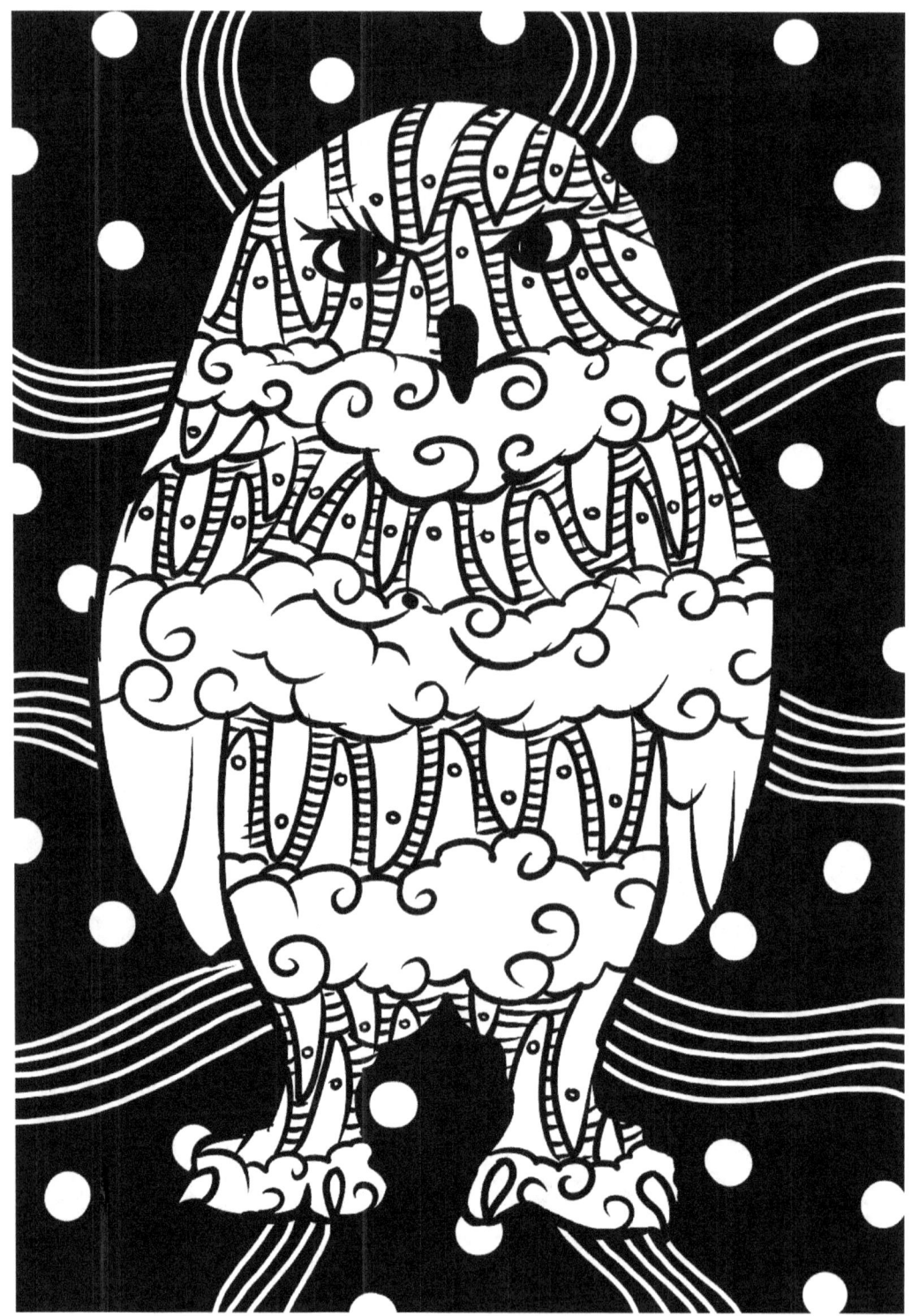

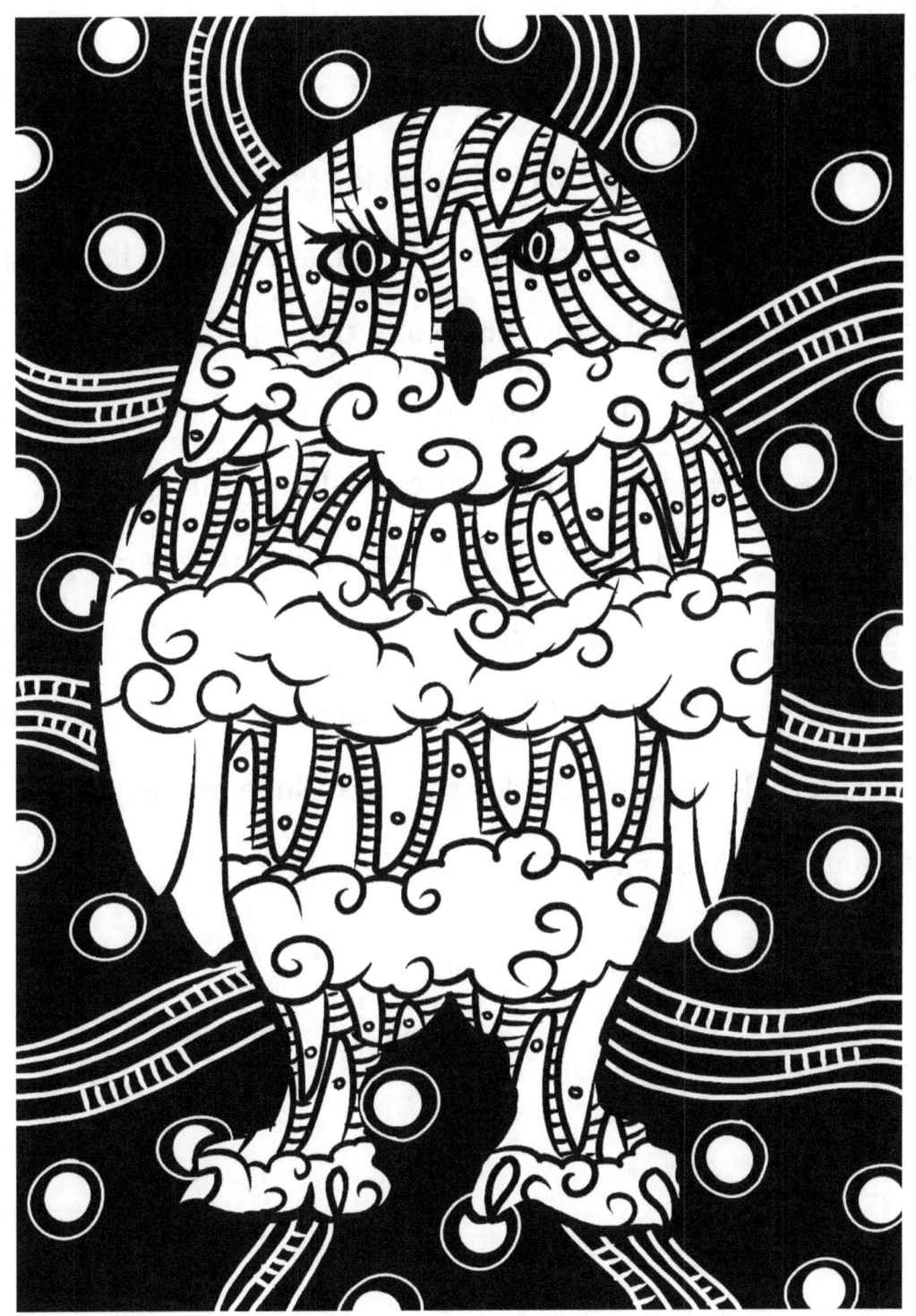

Doodle 4 – Parrot

In case you haven't picked up on the theme of these doodles yet let me help you out, it's all about animals. You can have a lot of fun if you set a specific theme and play to whatever it is. It makes for a very interesting drawing session and also helps expand your patterns and design capabilities. Taking a look at this parrot you'll notice that. Lot of ground gets covered pretty quickly. From the jump we have the base body and then we add the branch and ruffles of feathers and then we dive straight into the pattern. Keep following along the next three images and we'll see you on the next page.

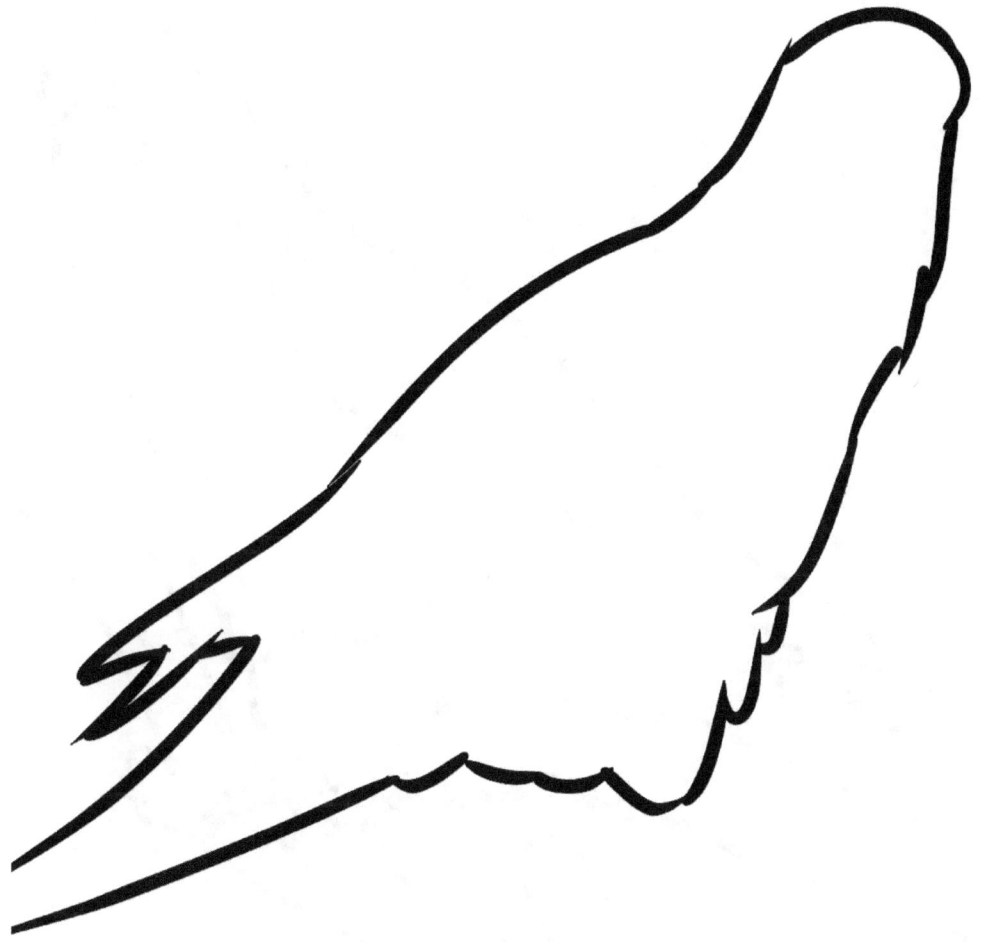

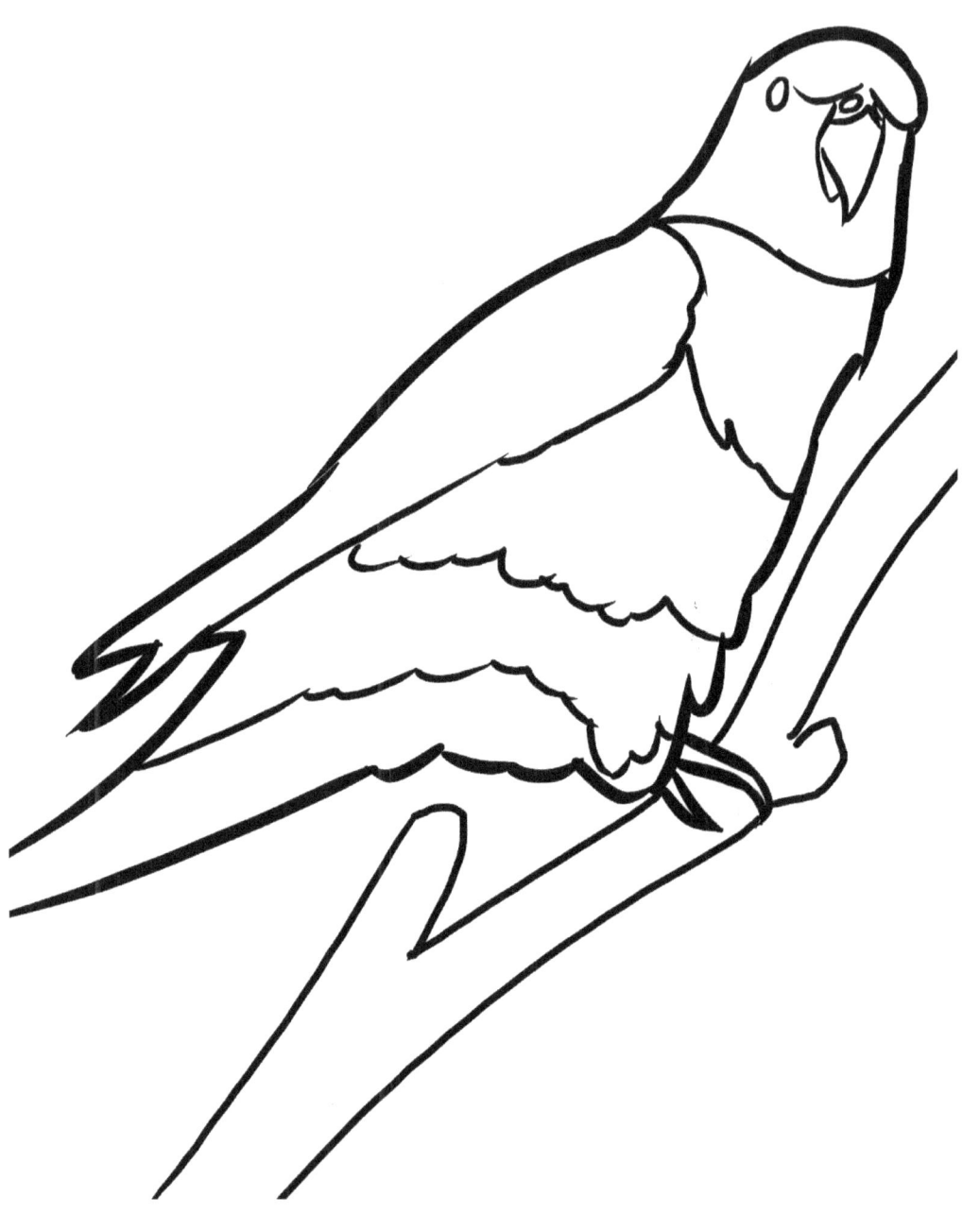

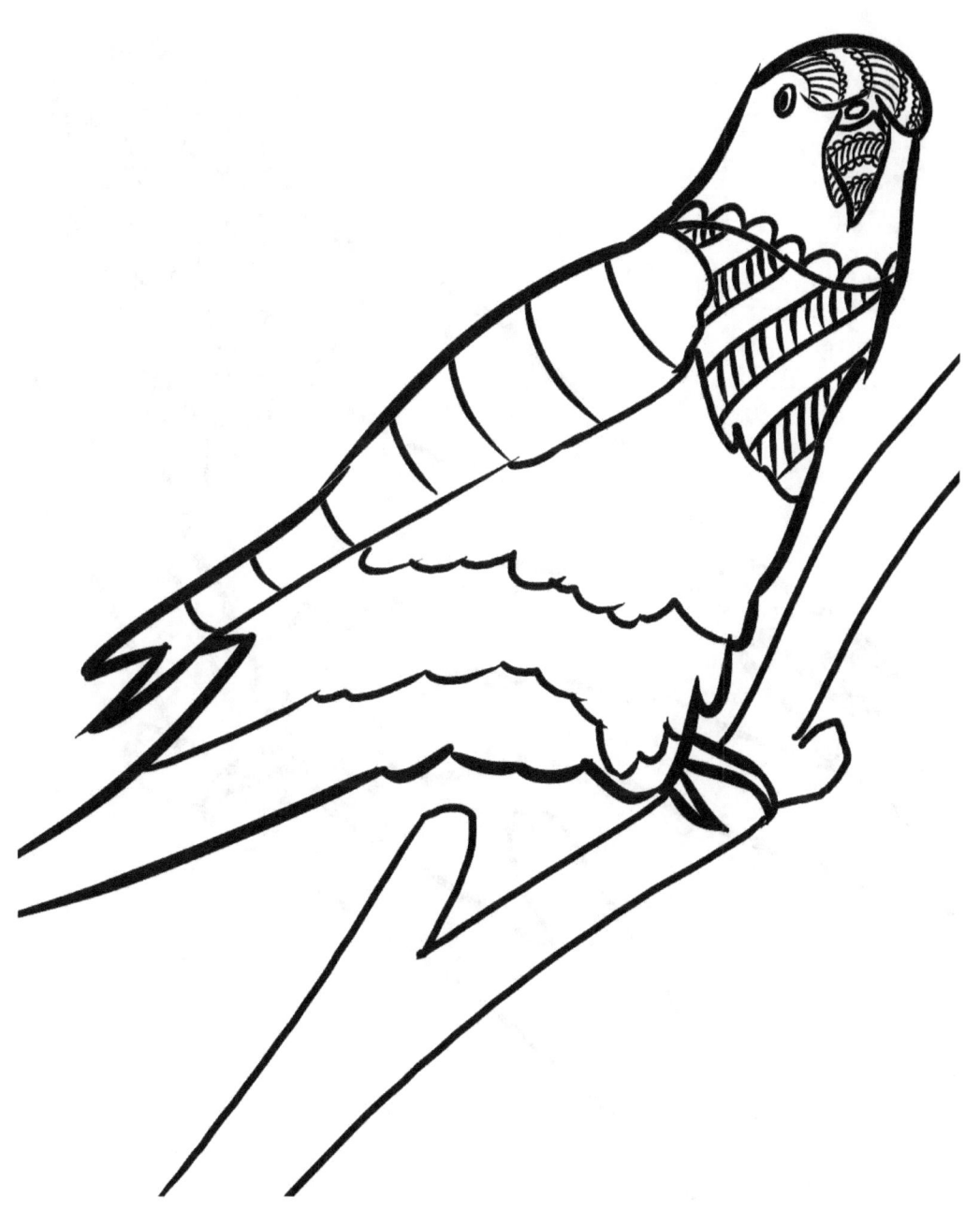

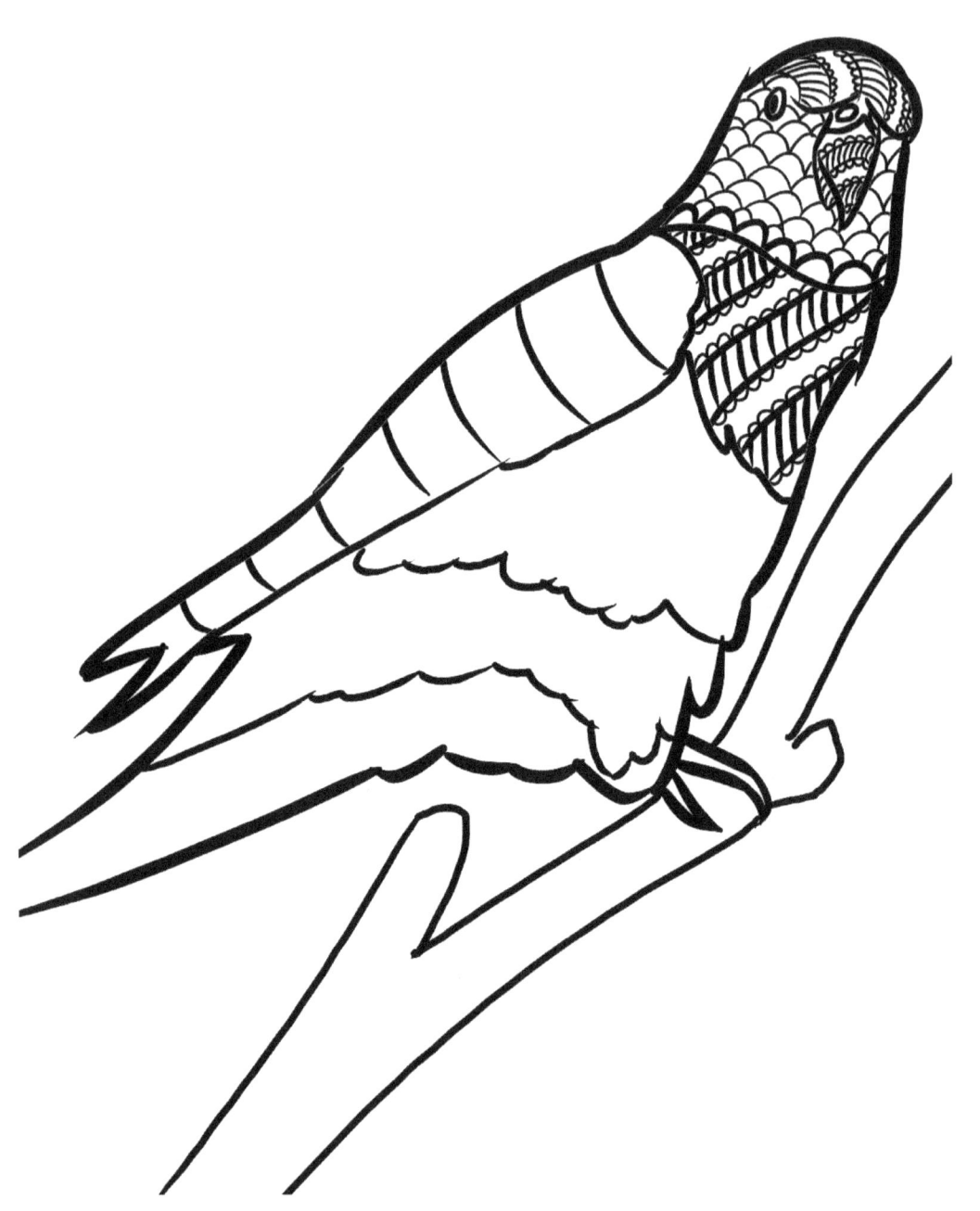

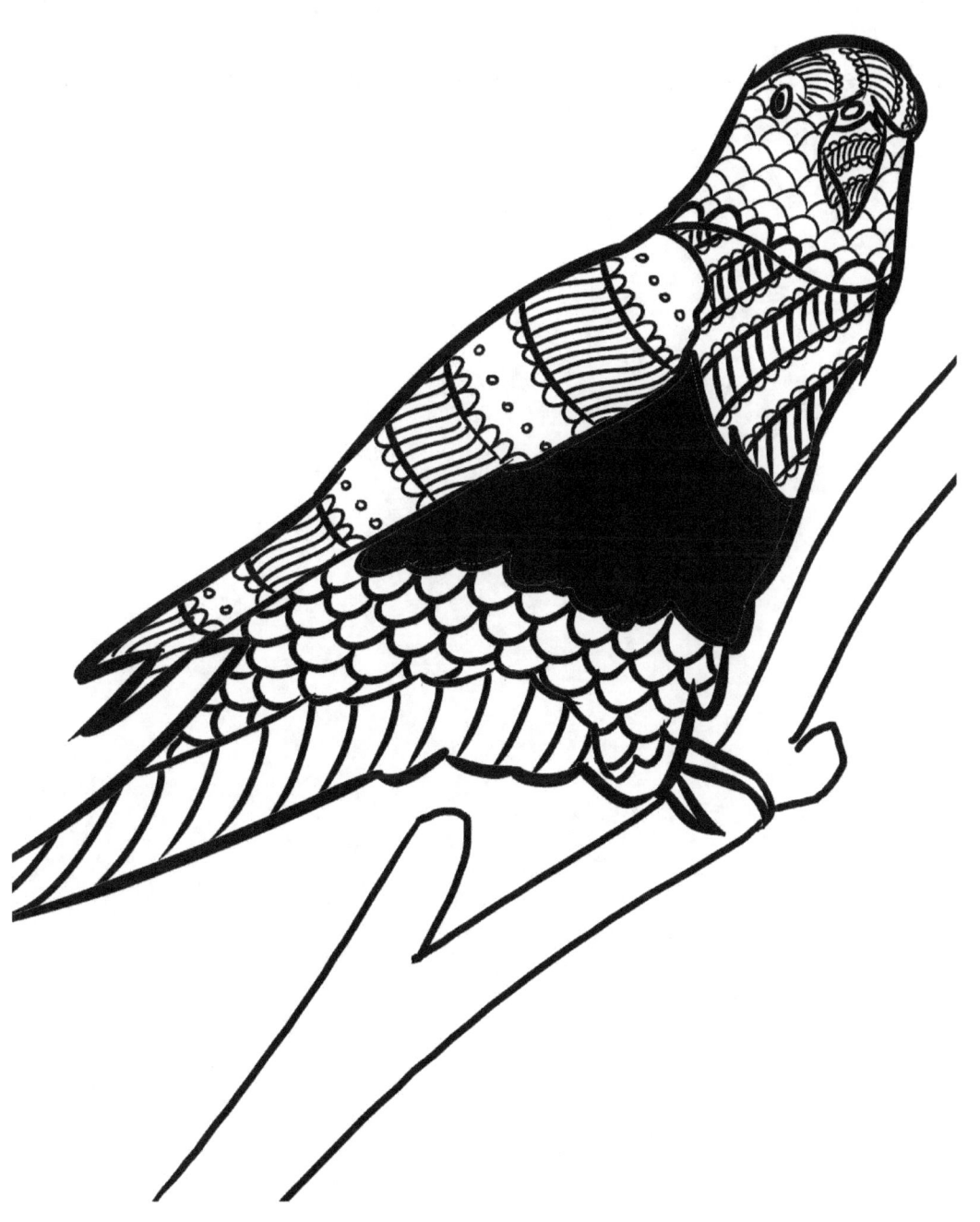

Now that we've delved into the shading you can see that the amount of detail in this specific piece isn't as great as the last one, yet the image itself is just as beautiful. Add the final touches as the seen in the last image below and then polish it up and call it finished!

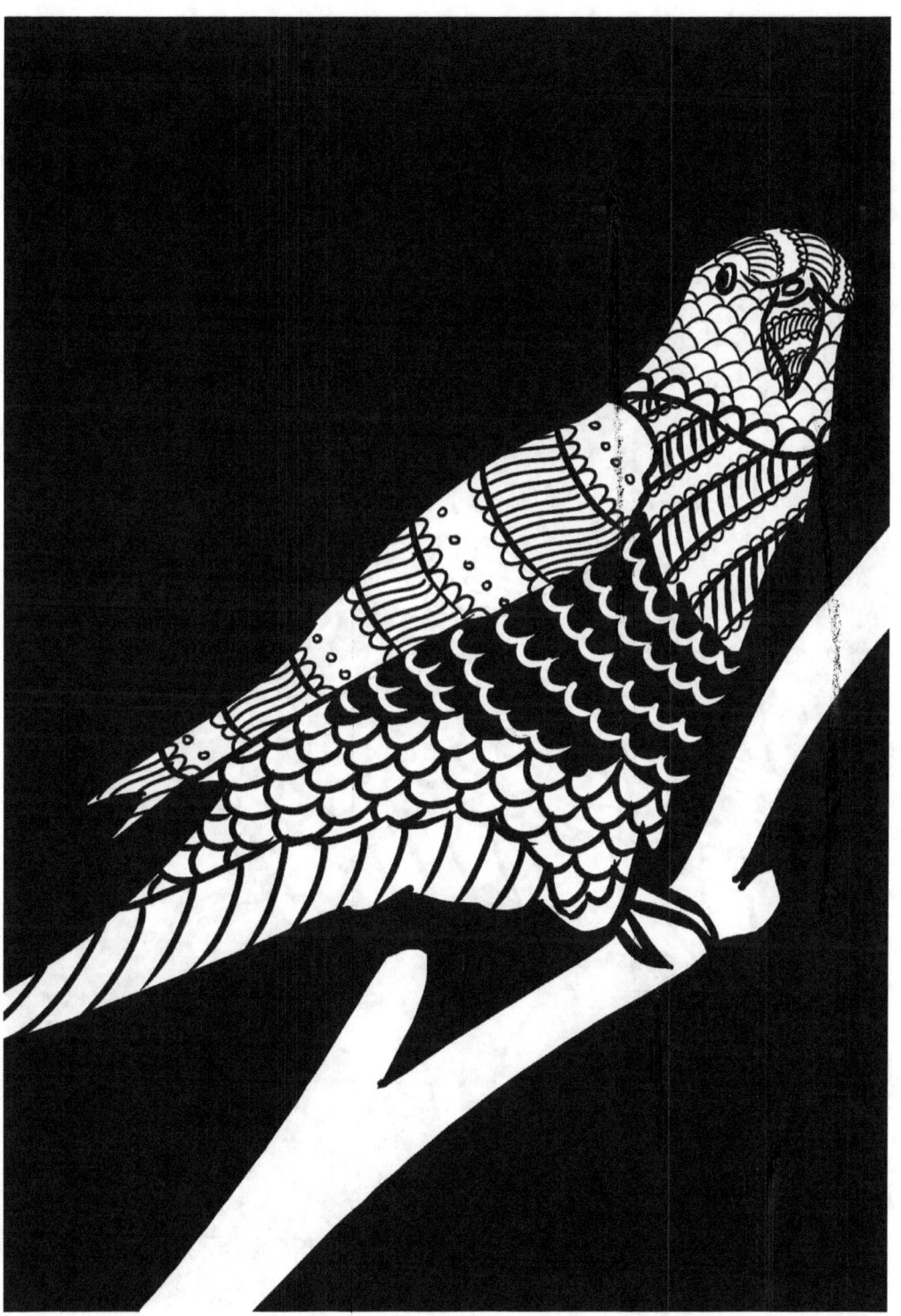

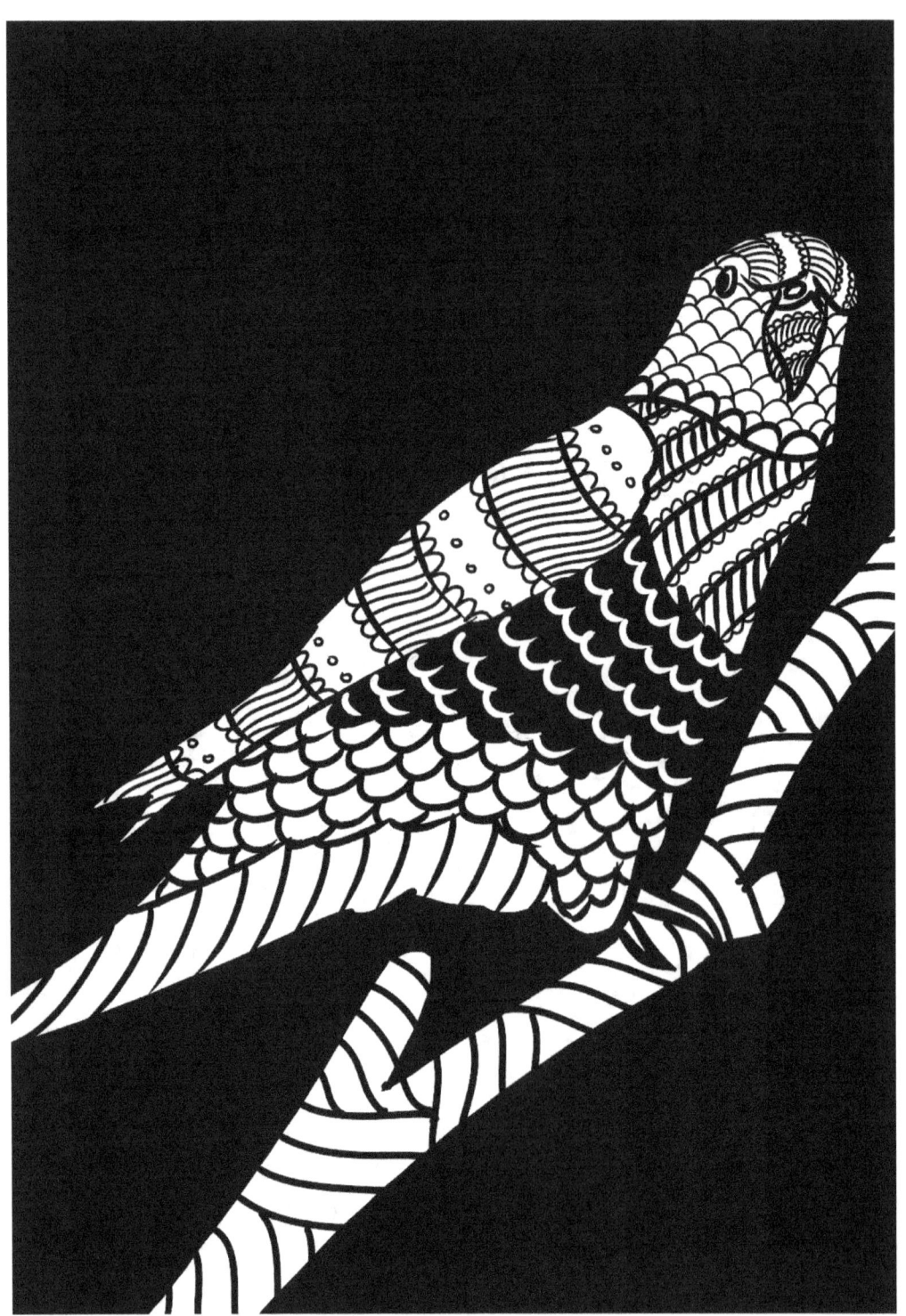

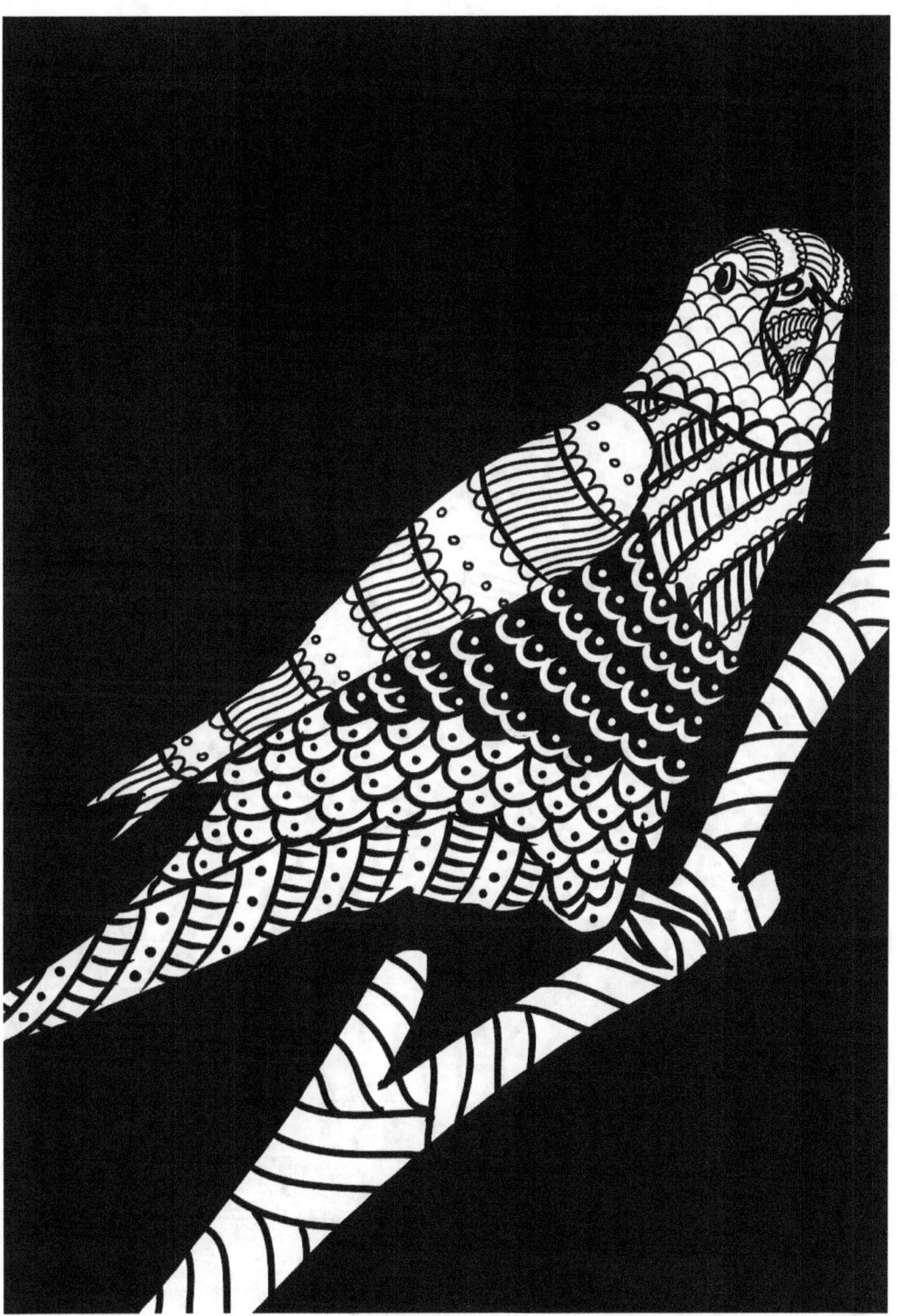

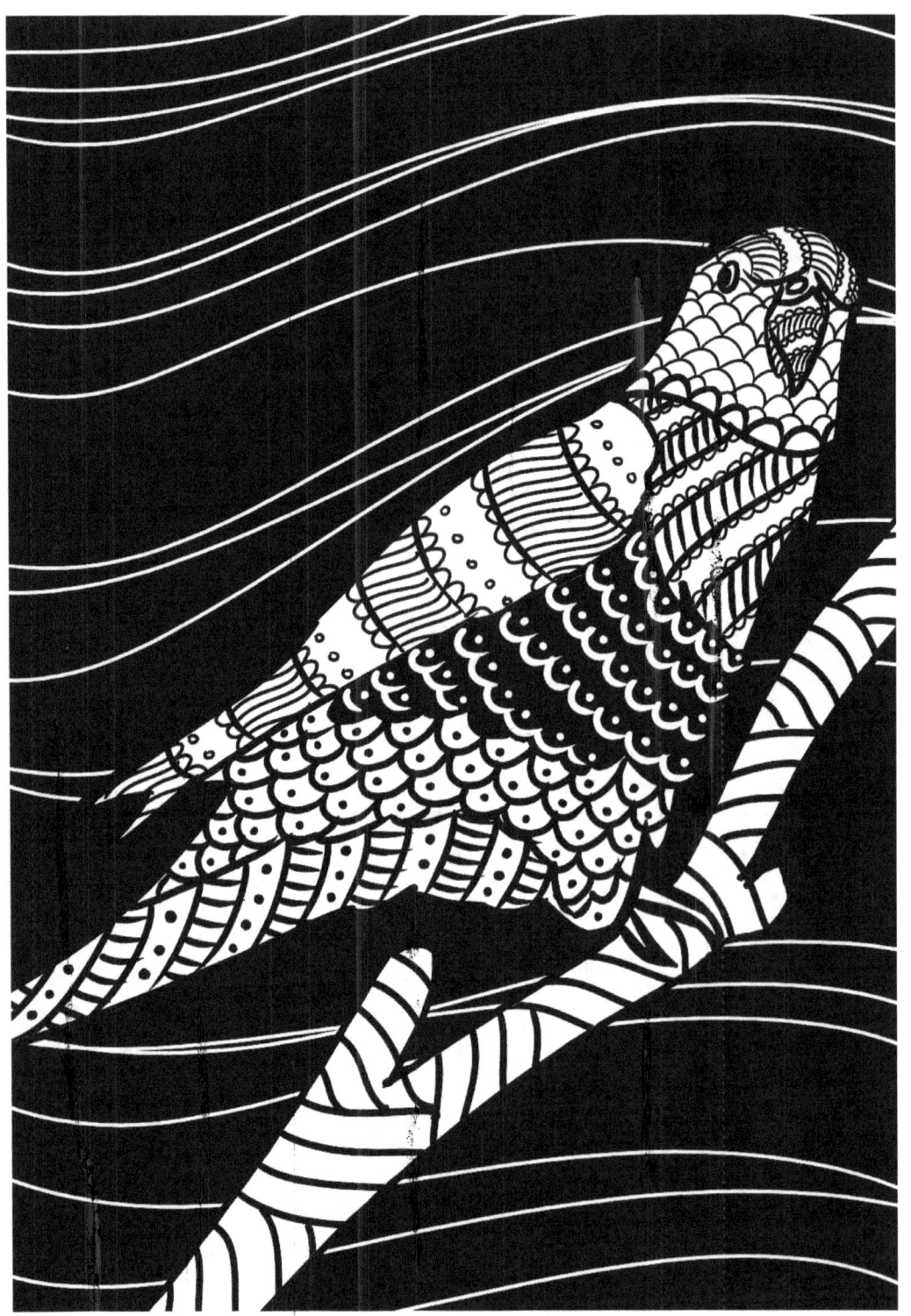

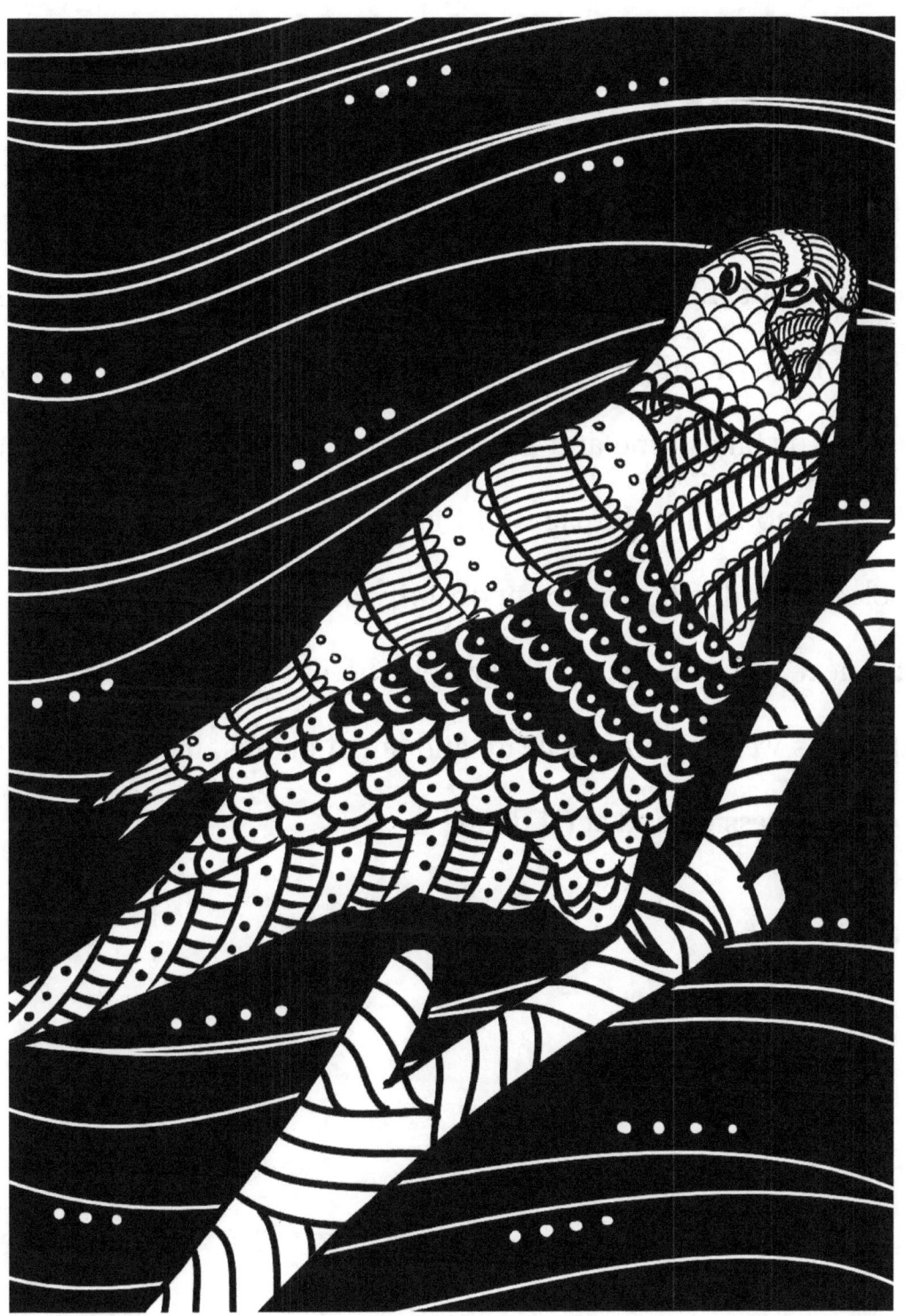

Doodle 5 – Wolf

With this next image you're going to see a lot of the wave patterns put into play, just as a heads up. The thing to keep in mind is to manipulate the patterns to your own needs and desires. It takes time and practice but as you already learned in the first 20 some odd pages of this book, it's possible! So take a look at this doodle as an opportunity and proceed forward into the next three images with grace! There's a lot of shading up ahead as well as some delicate and small details, have no fear in your progression and get it done.

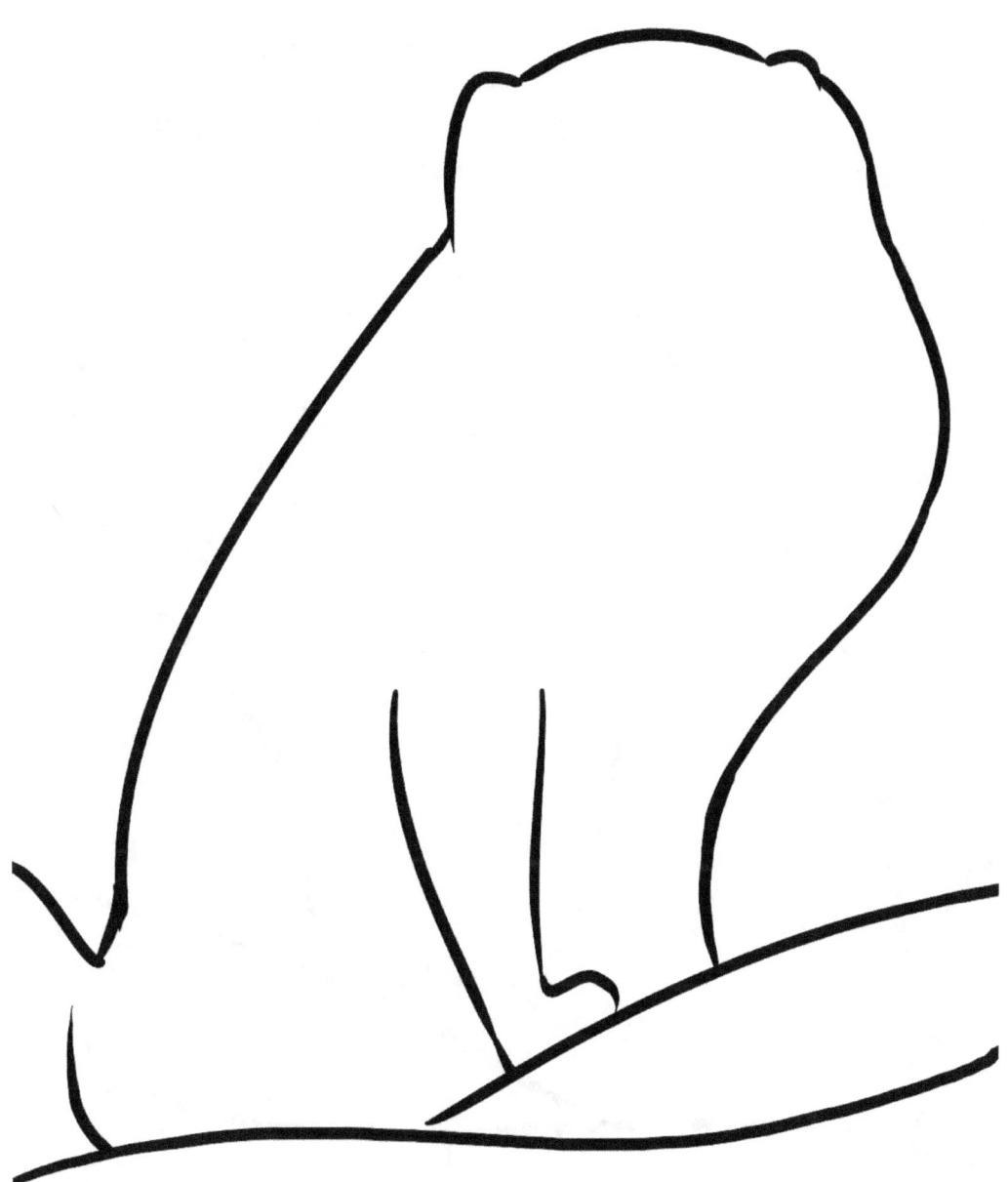

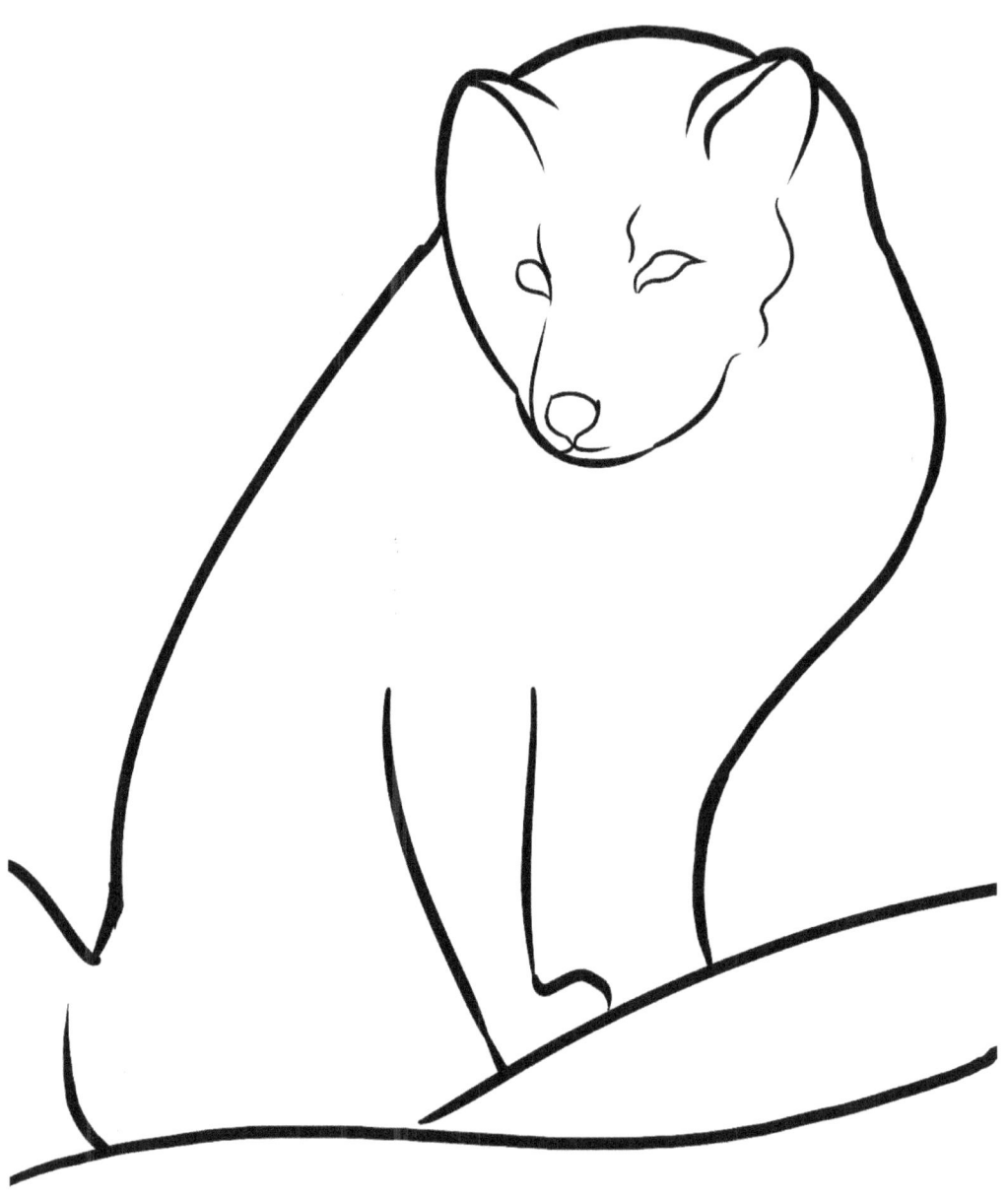

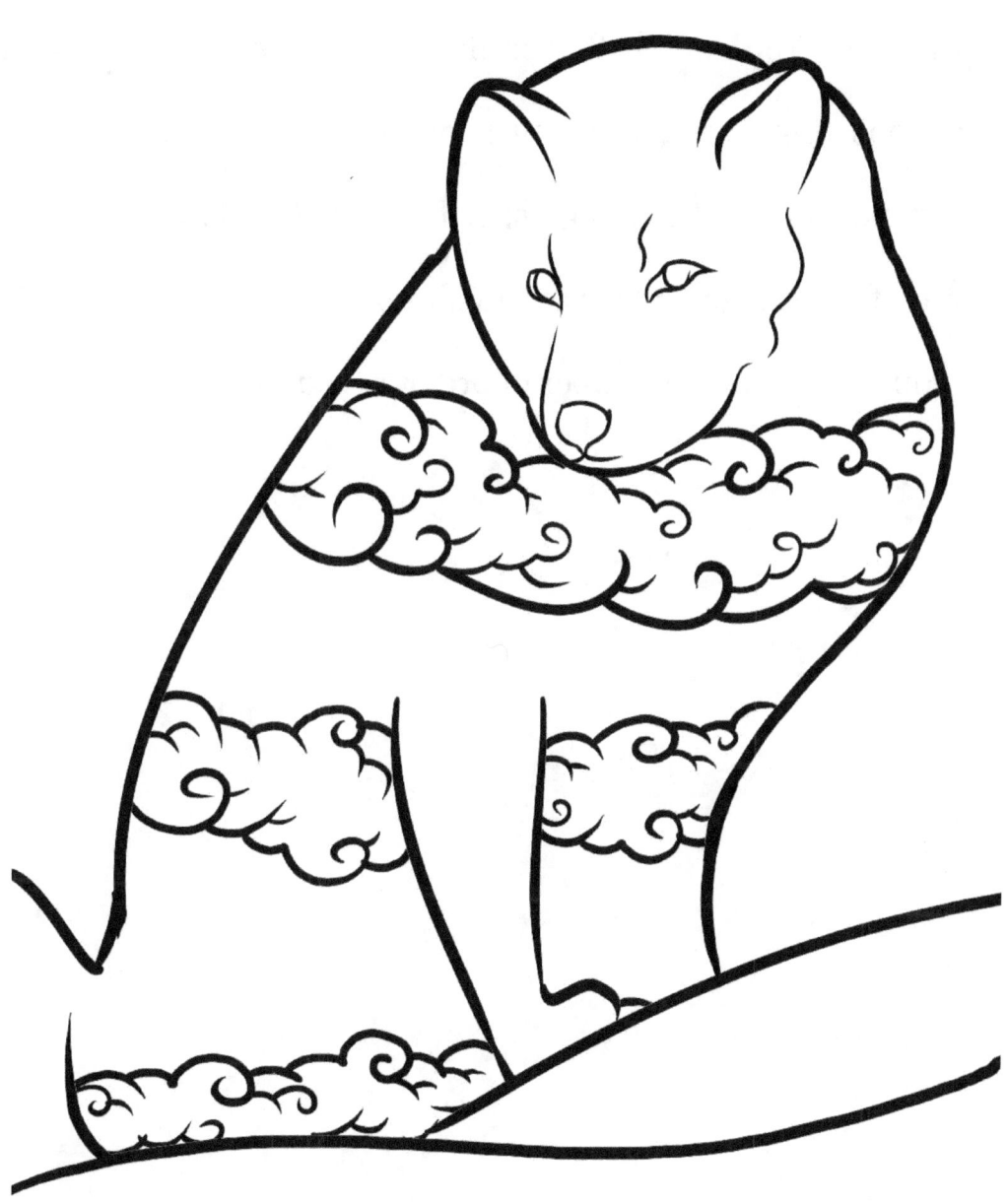

Now you have the finished product here before you! How does it look? You can really see the wave patterns in full force here. Good thing we got so much practice in earlier. The most delicate portion of this image specifically would have to be the bottom of the image. So as you finish up your version of it make sure you keep that in as proper of order as you can.

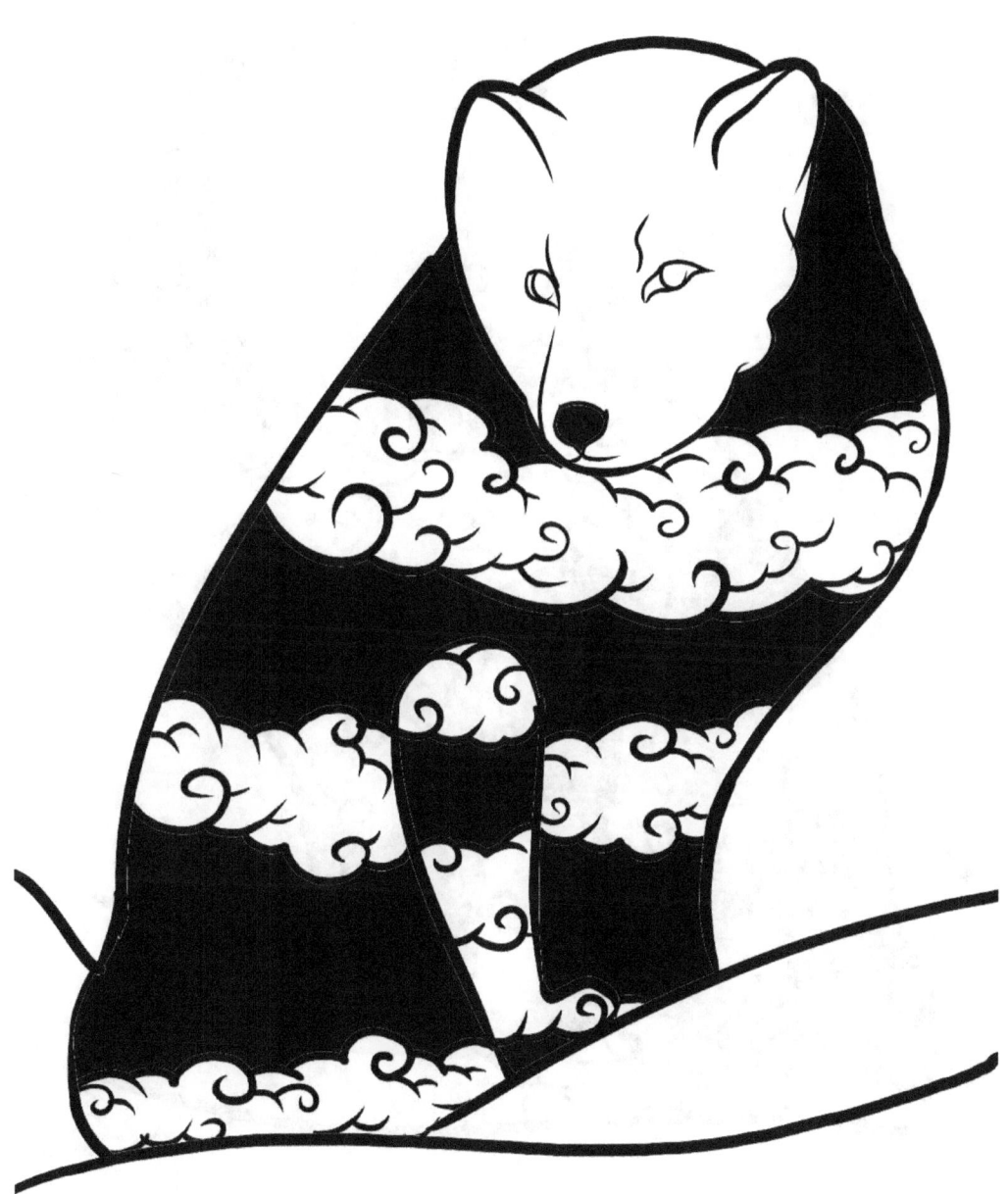

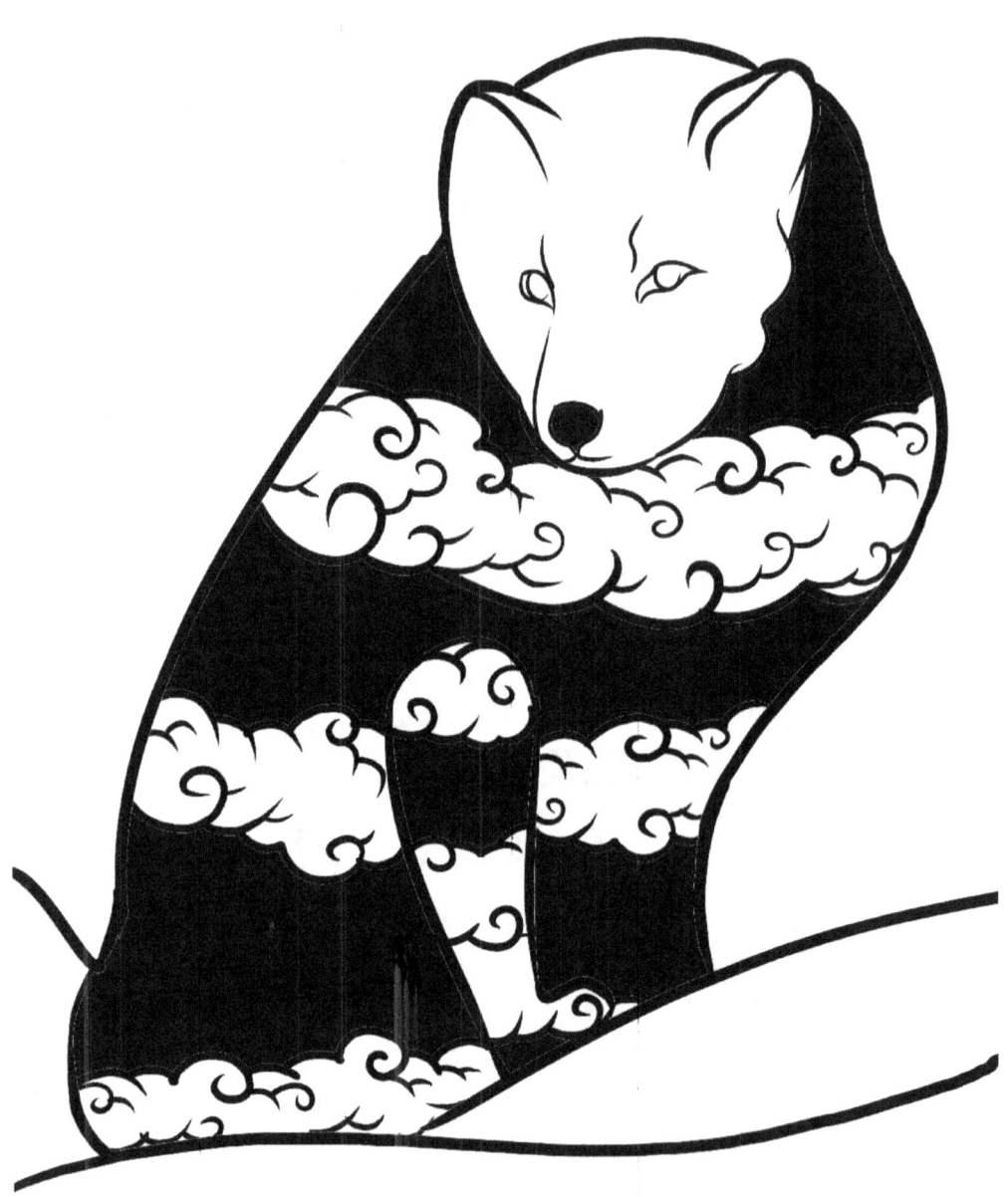

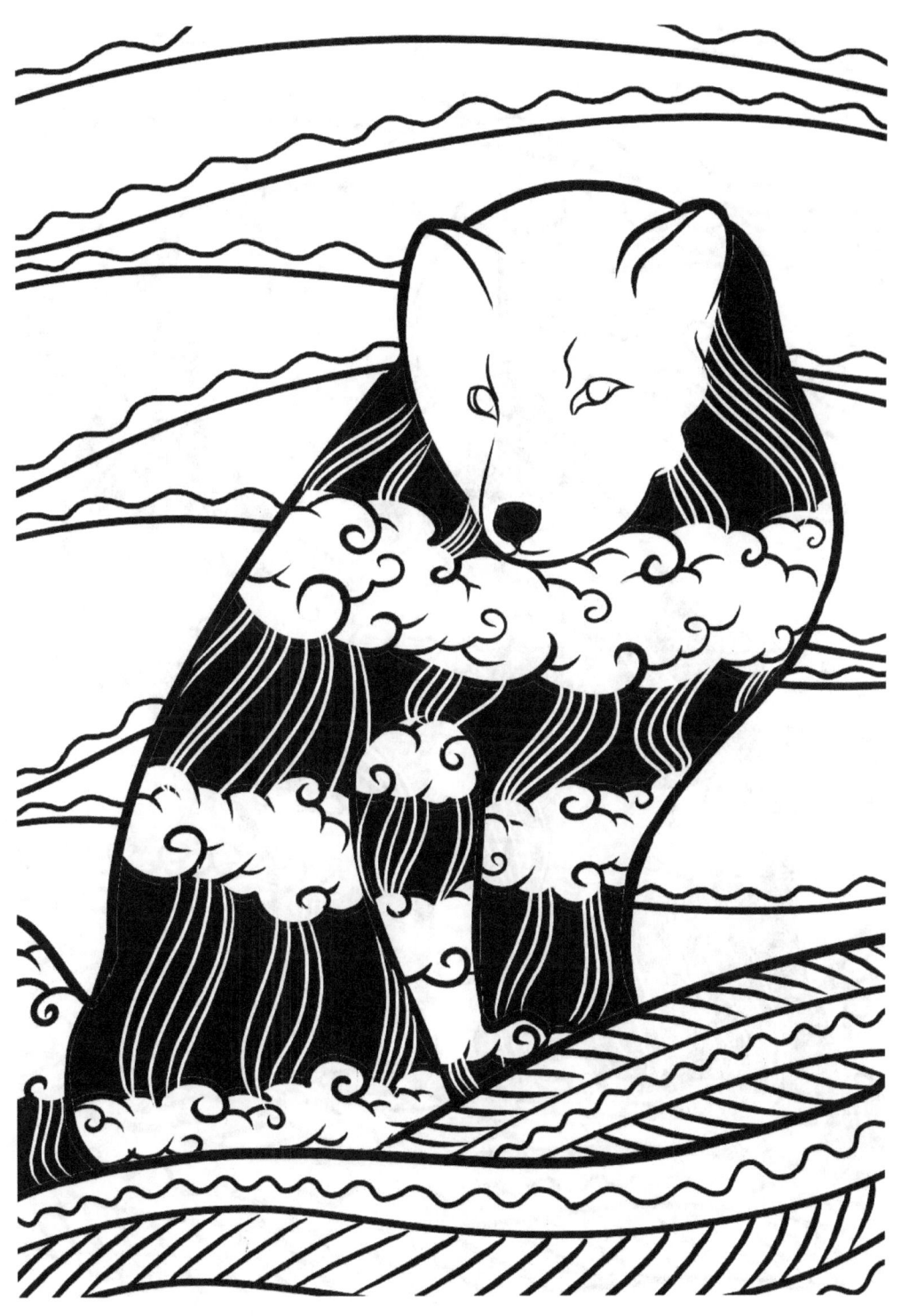

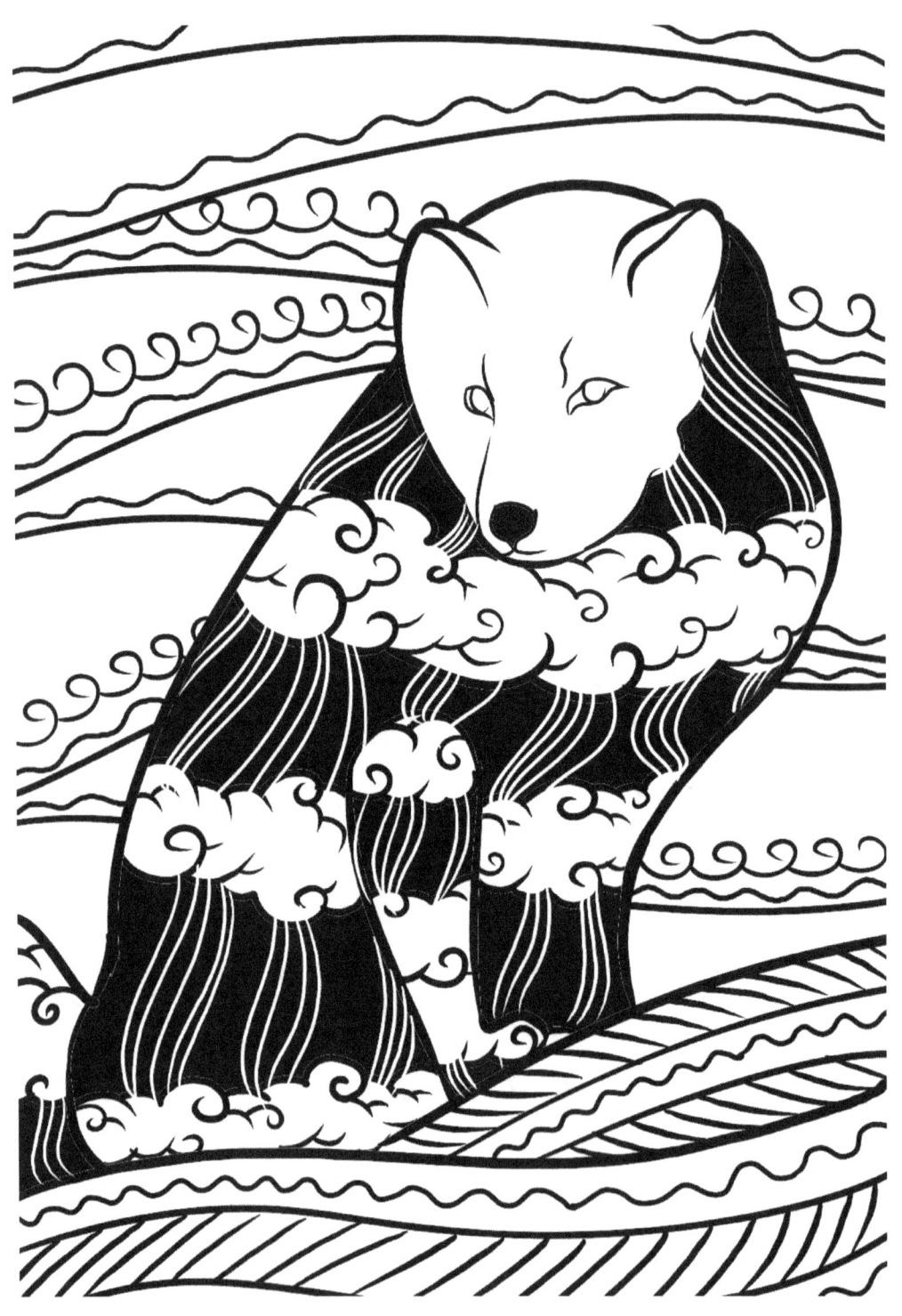

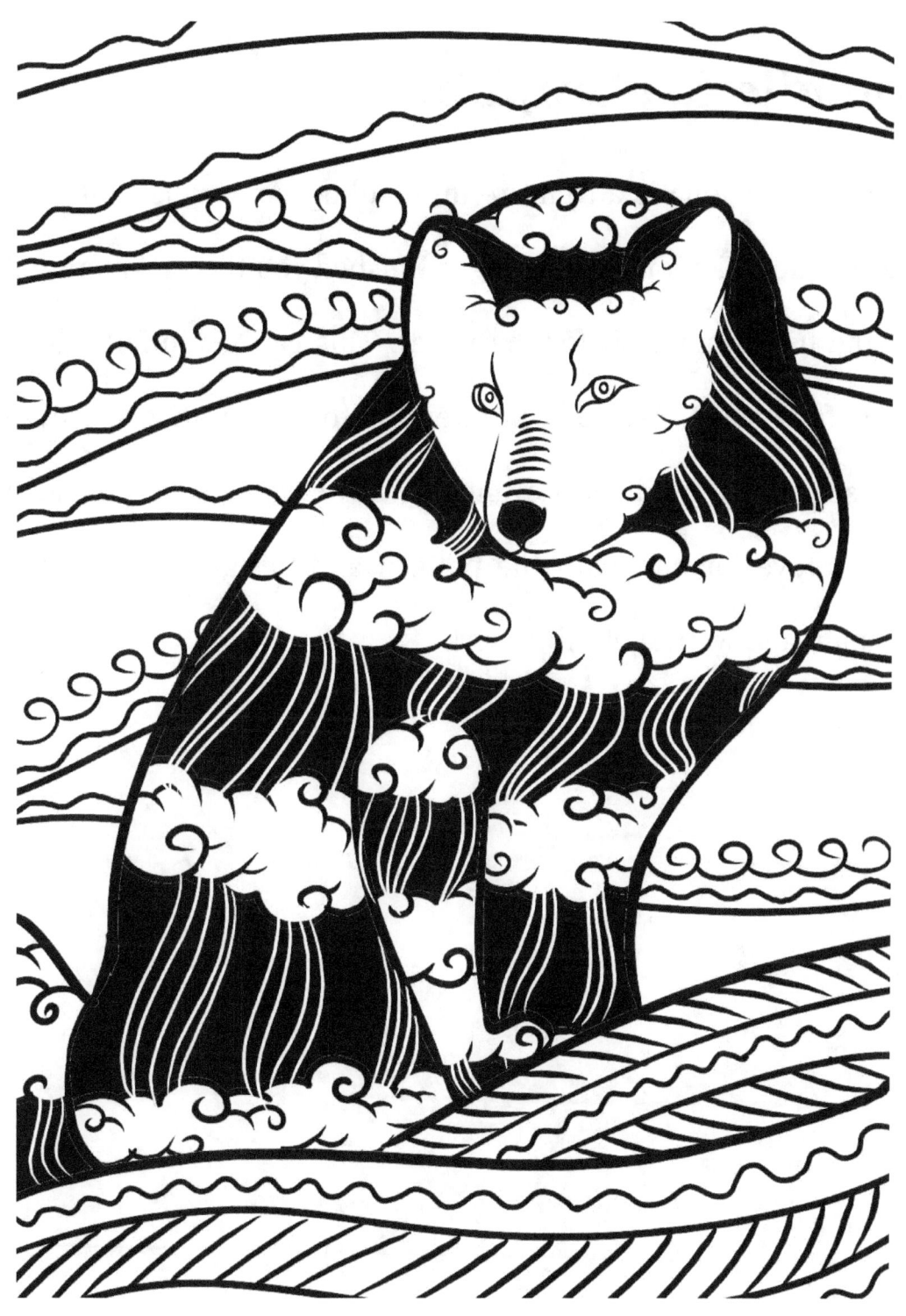

Doodle 6 – Dolphin

Time for an aquatic adventure in doodling. As you see, once the basic foundation of the drawing is finished you then segment half of the background off for the water. This can potentially throw you off so make sure you pay attention to the negative space. All the space will be filled in eventually anyways so have no fear of that. Move forward with the pattern and design on the actual dolphin and watch your line work.

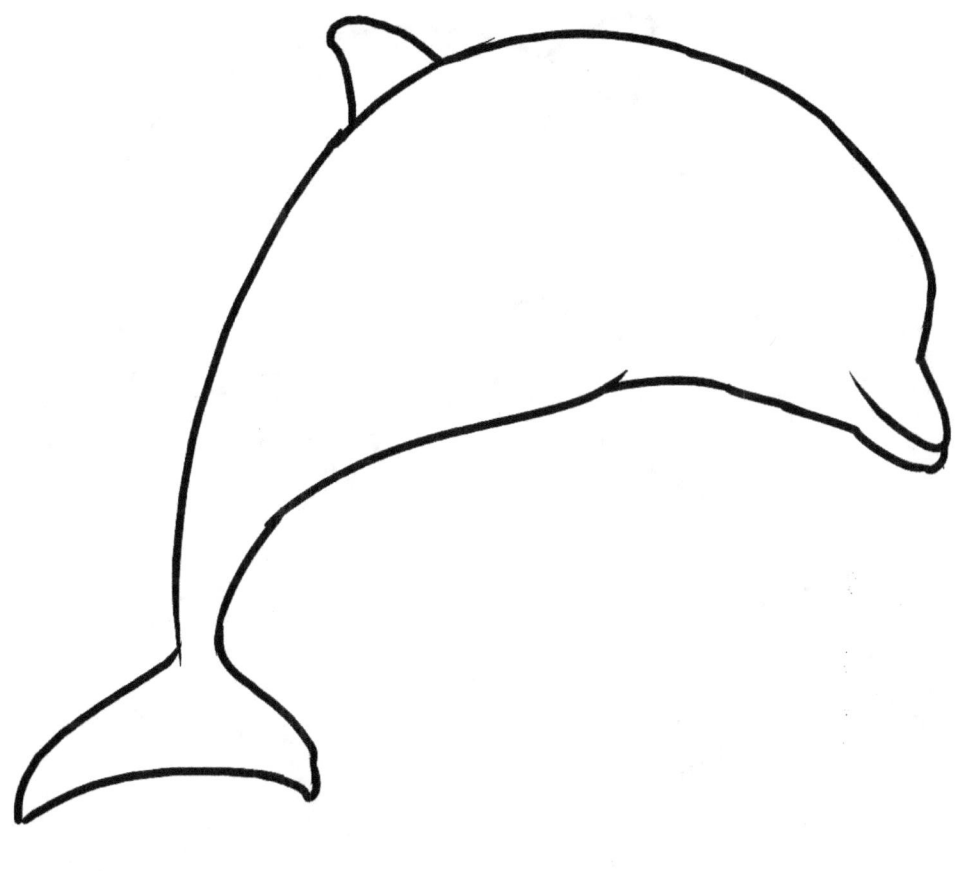

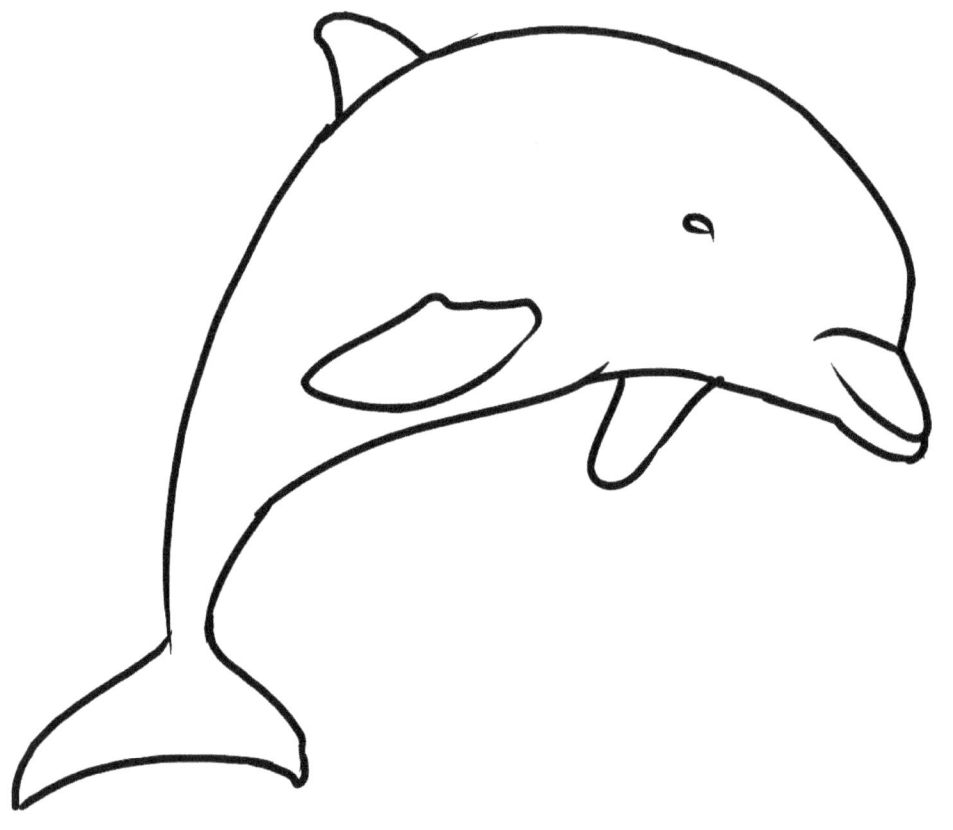

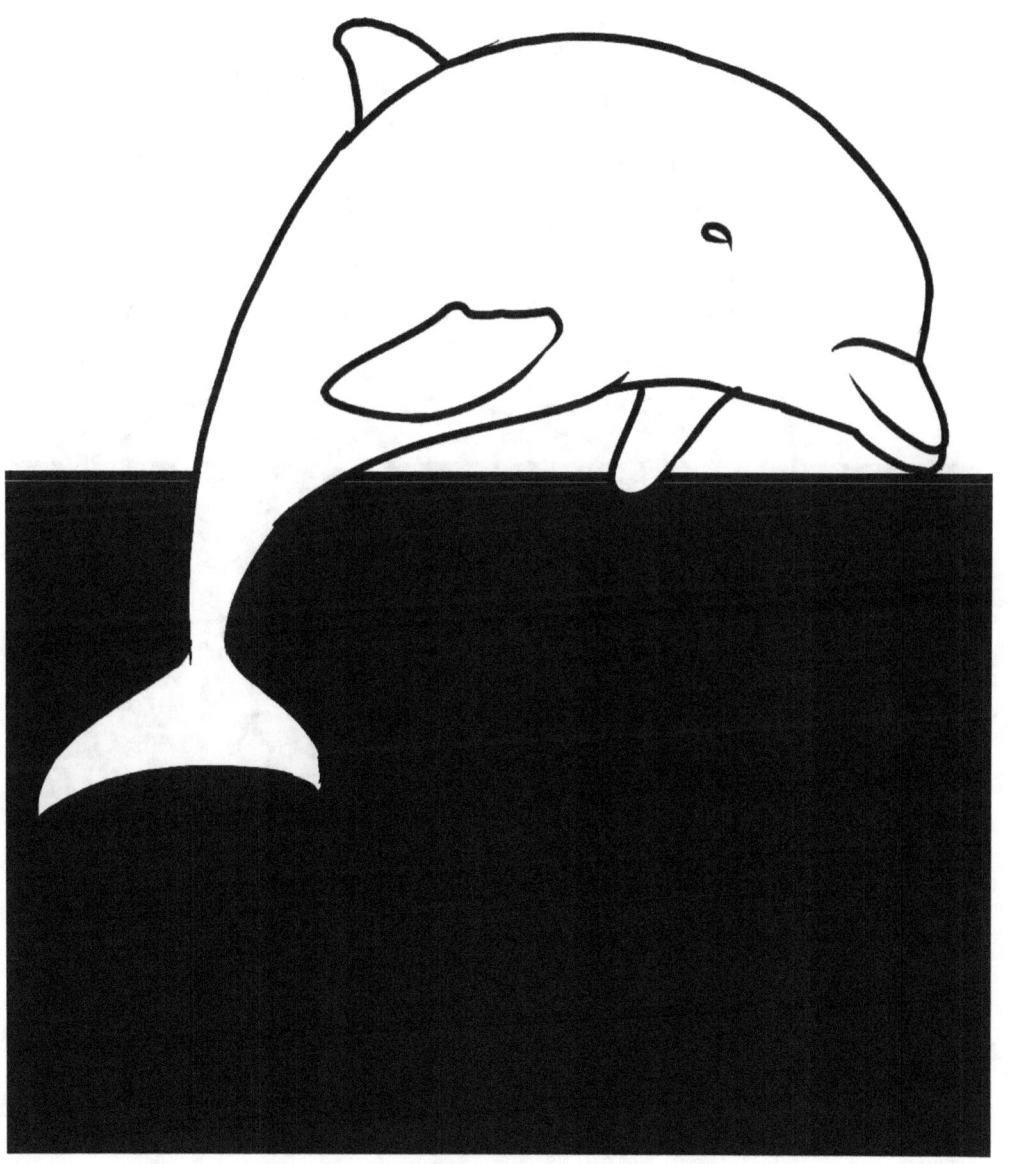

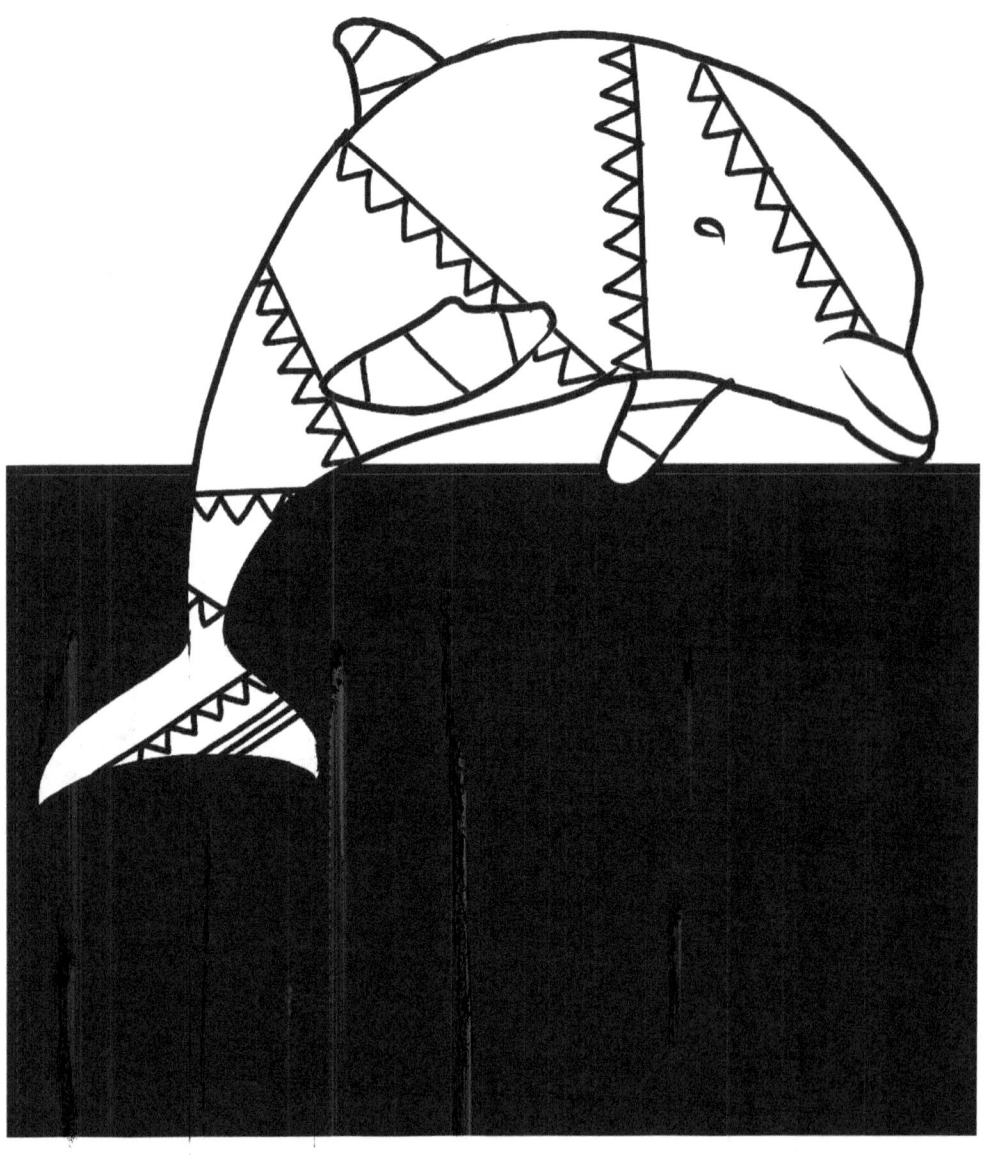

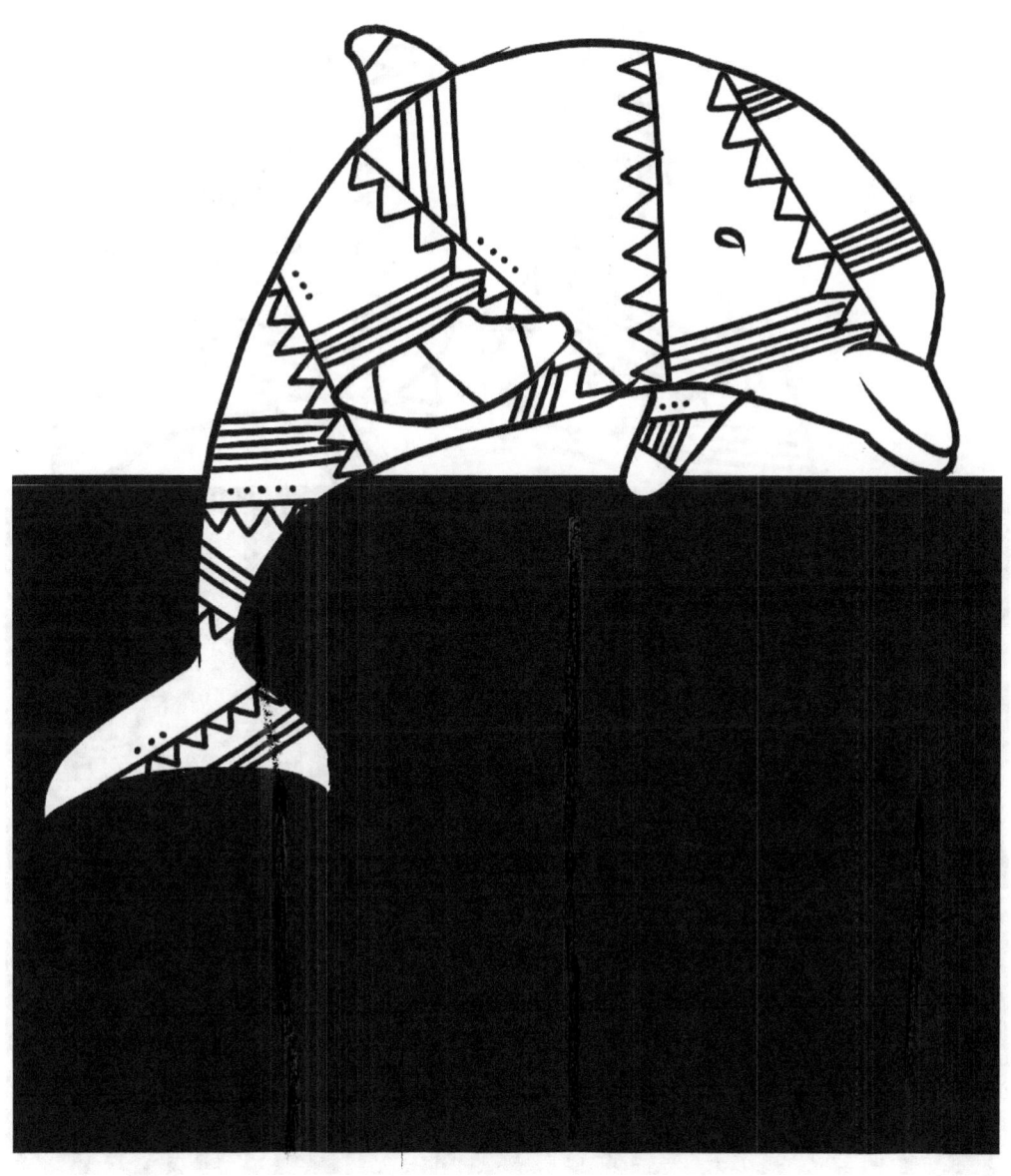

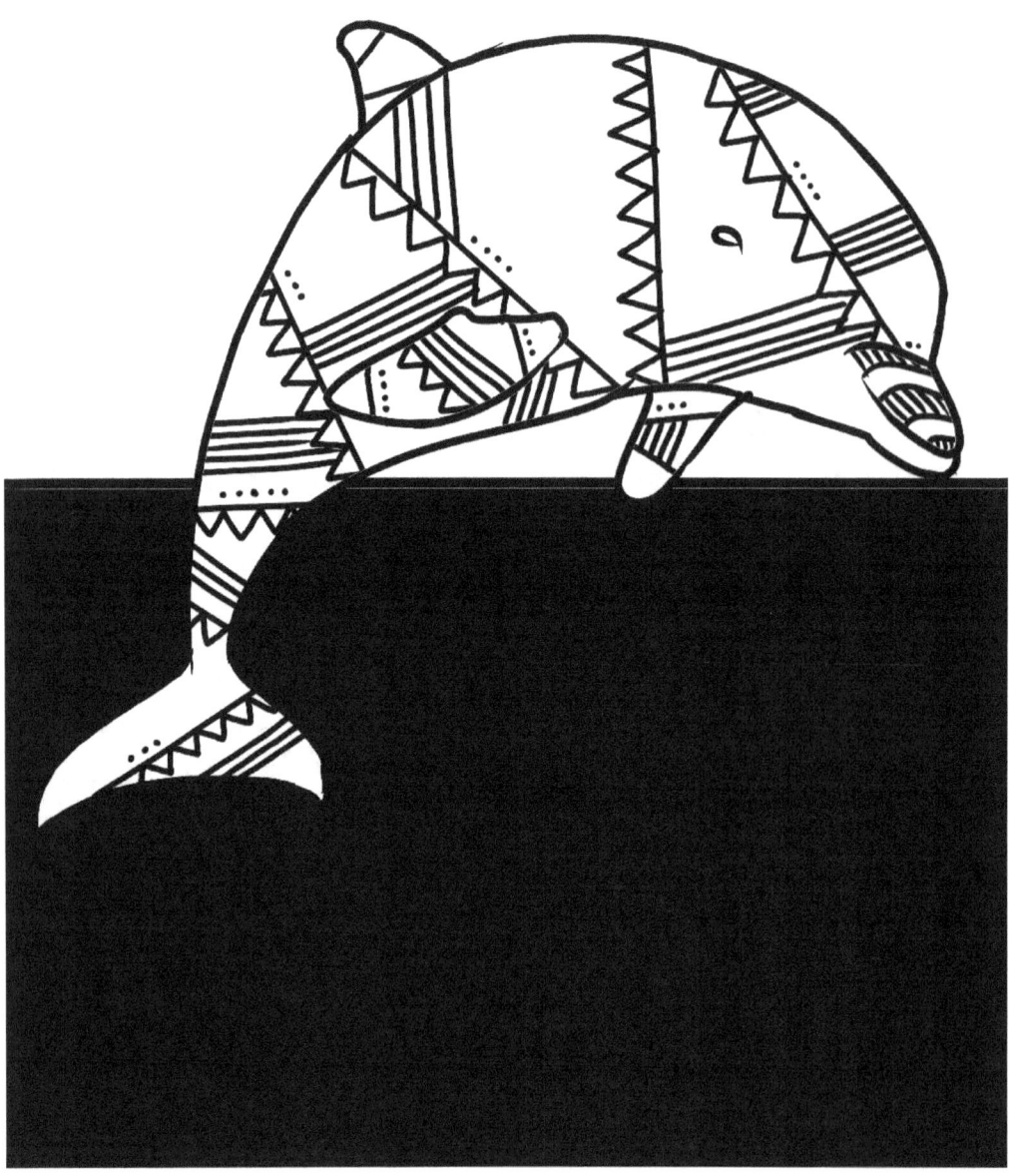

As promised you can see that both sides of the negative space, the black and the white, are being put to use in a very intricate and beautiful fashion. The line work is almost parallel yet opposite. You can see the smooth and wavy upper lines then the sharper and jagged edges below. That is something to pay close attention to as you finish up this image in the last couple steps. This is a good opportunity to get really comfortable with your shading abilities as well, so keep that in mind and move on to the final doodle when finished!

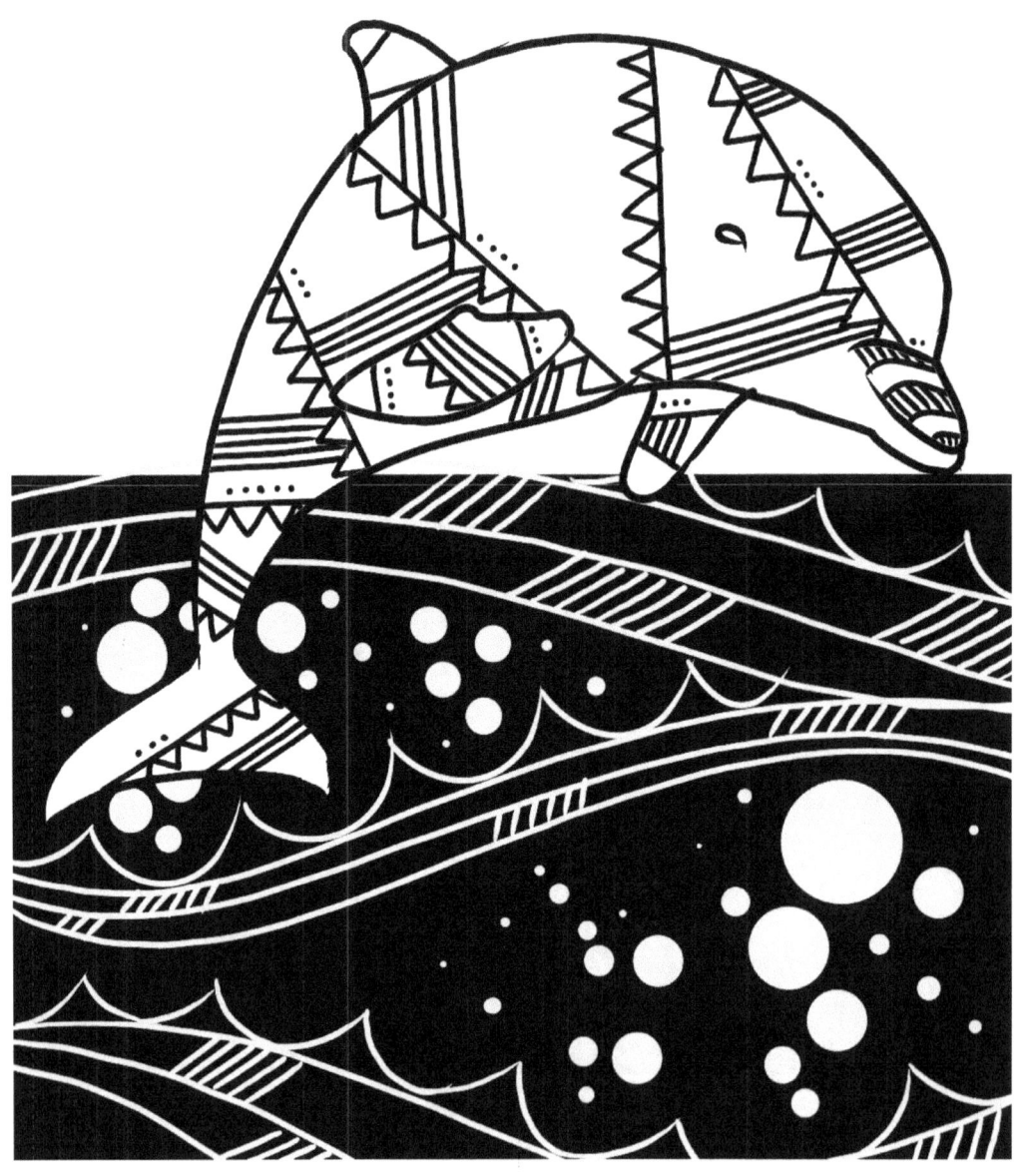

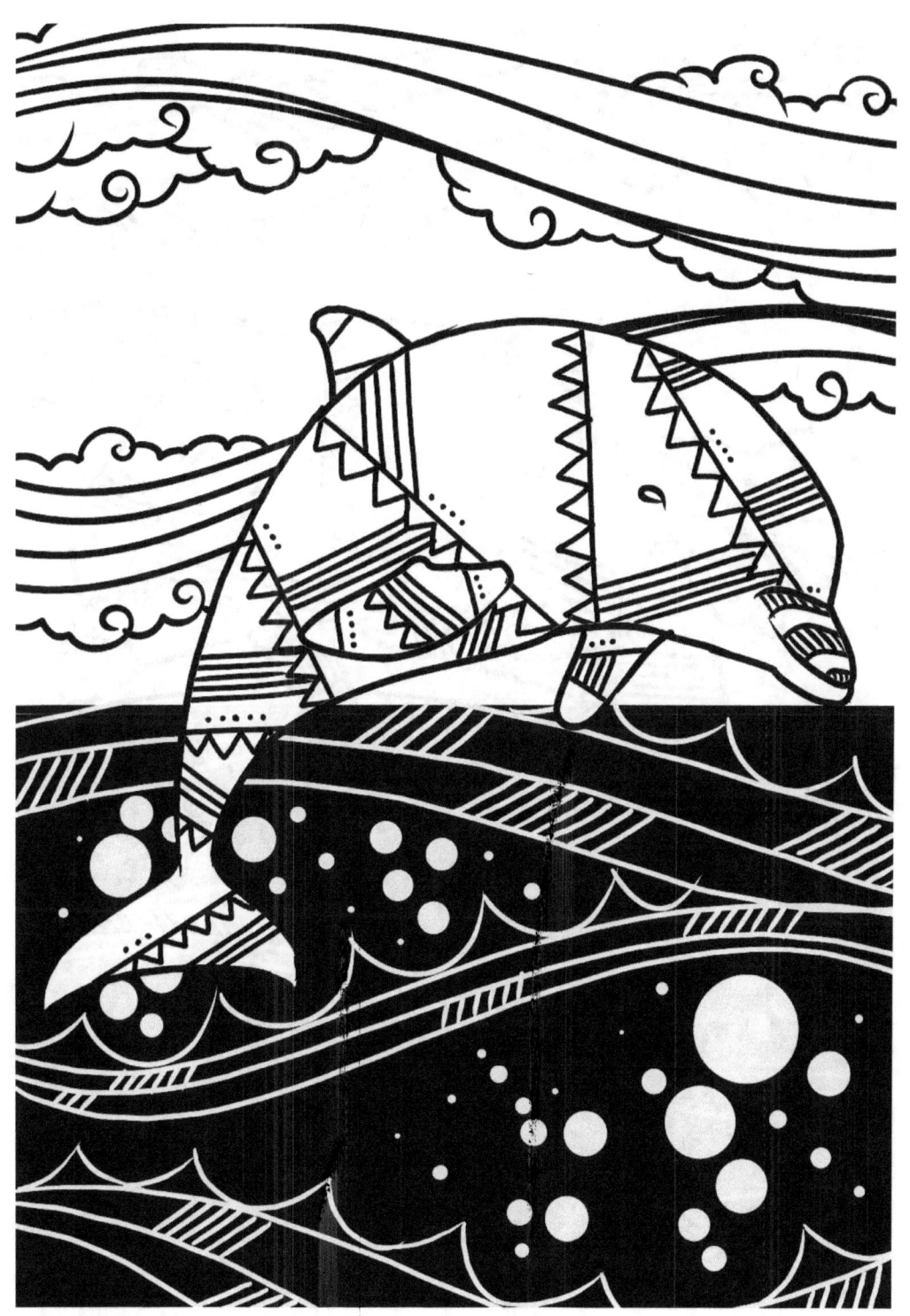

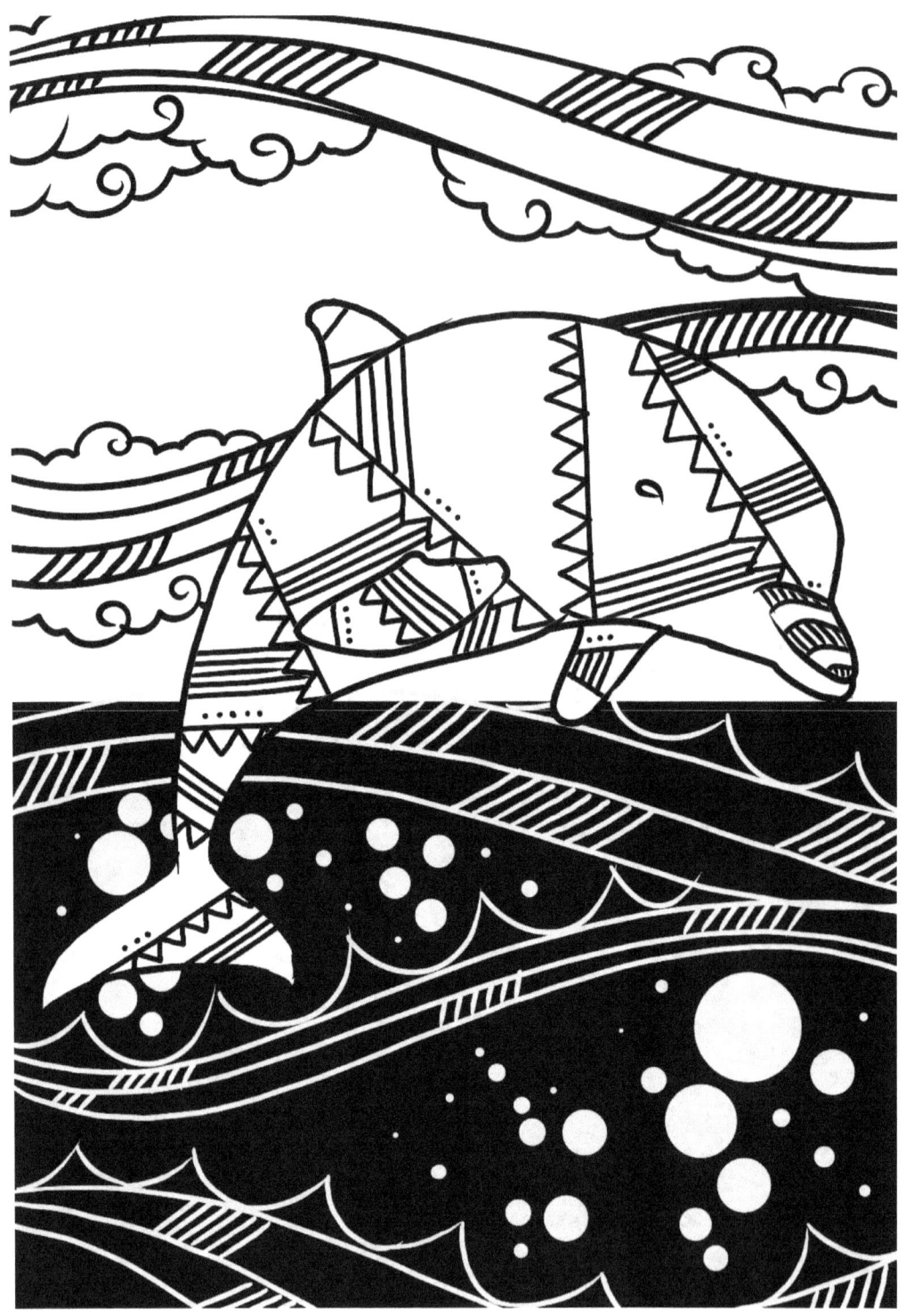

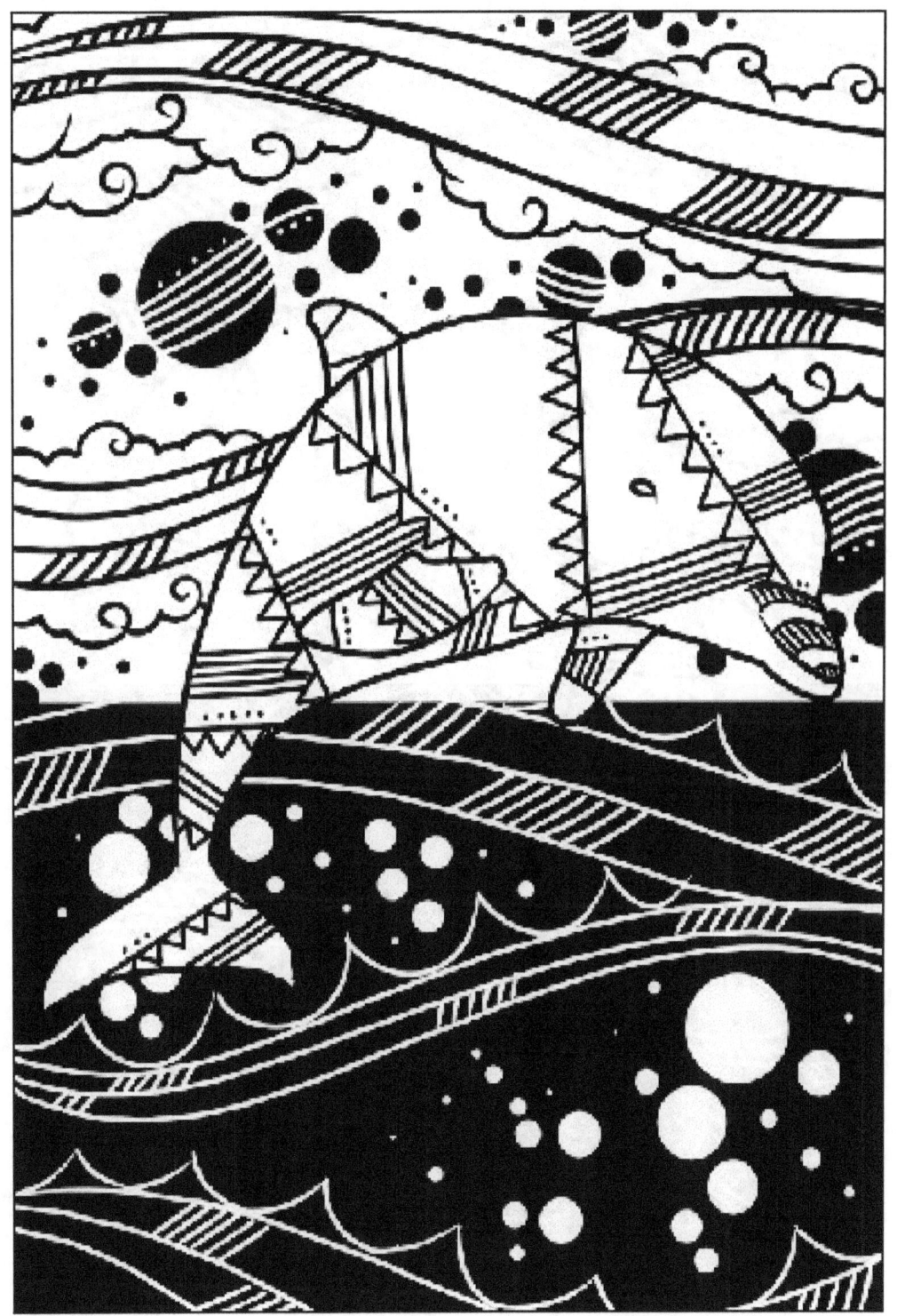

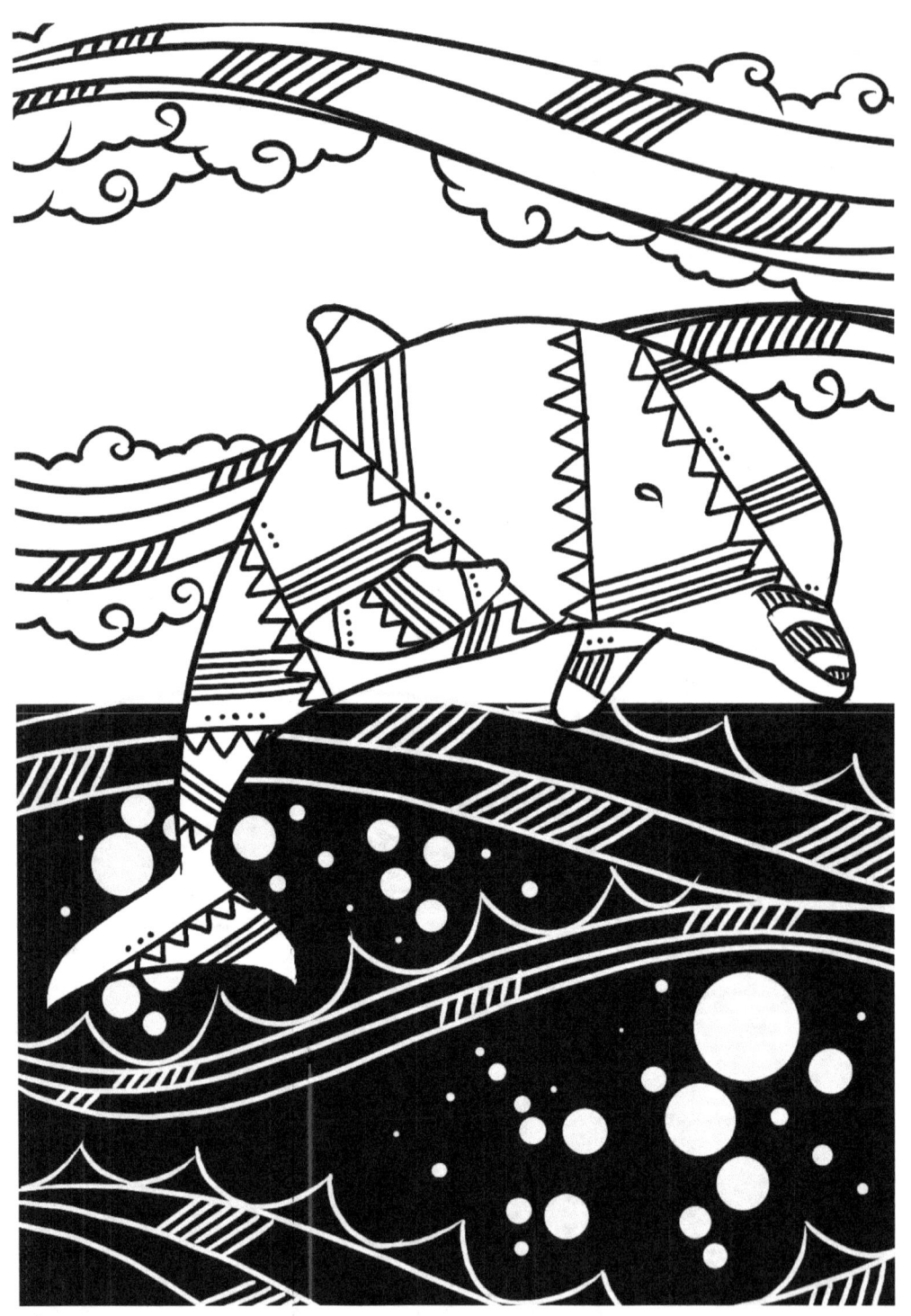

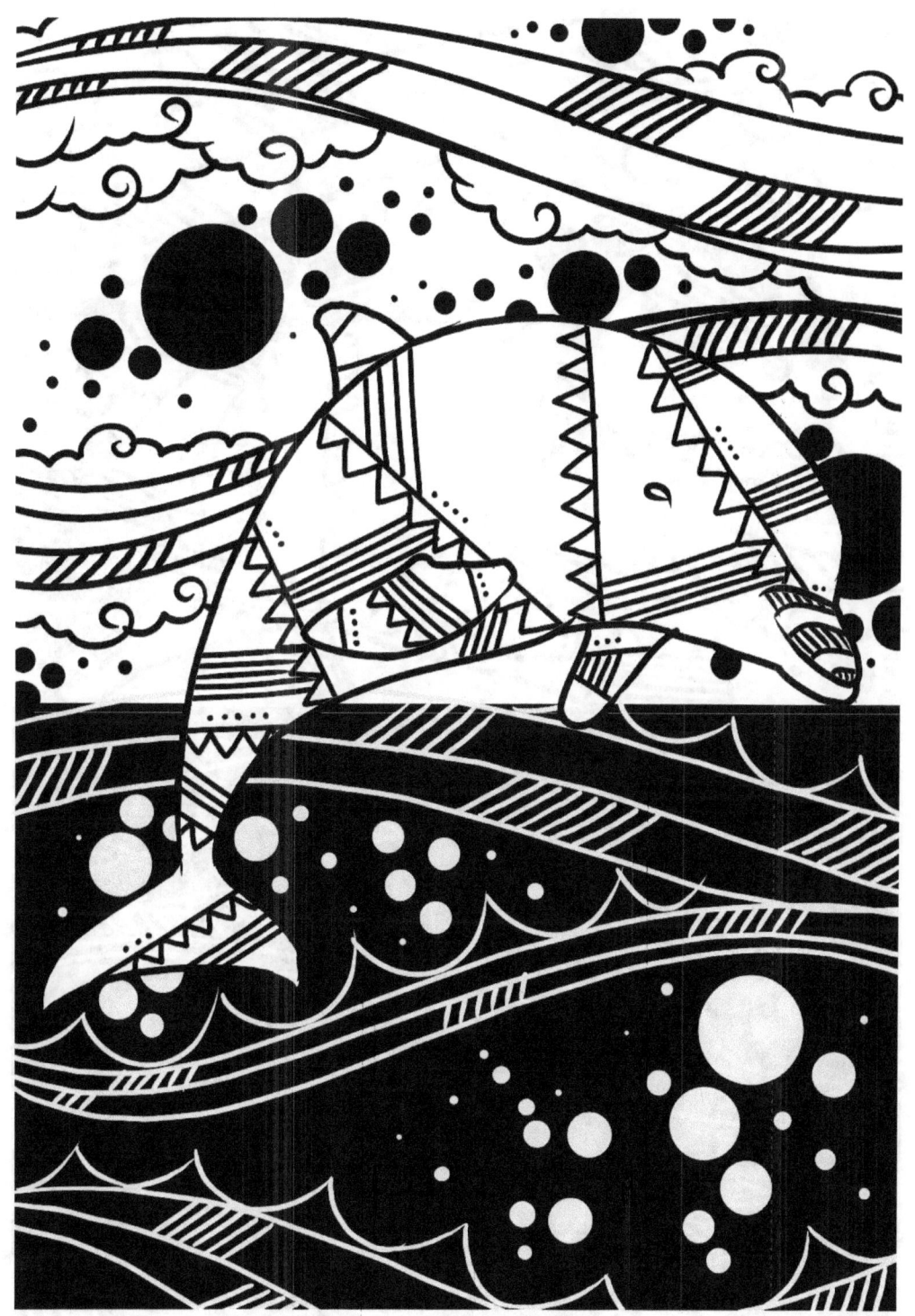

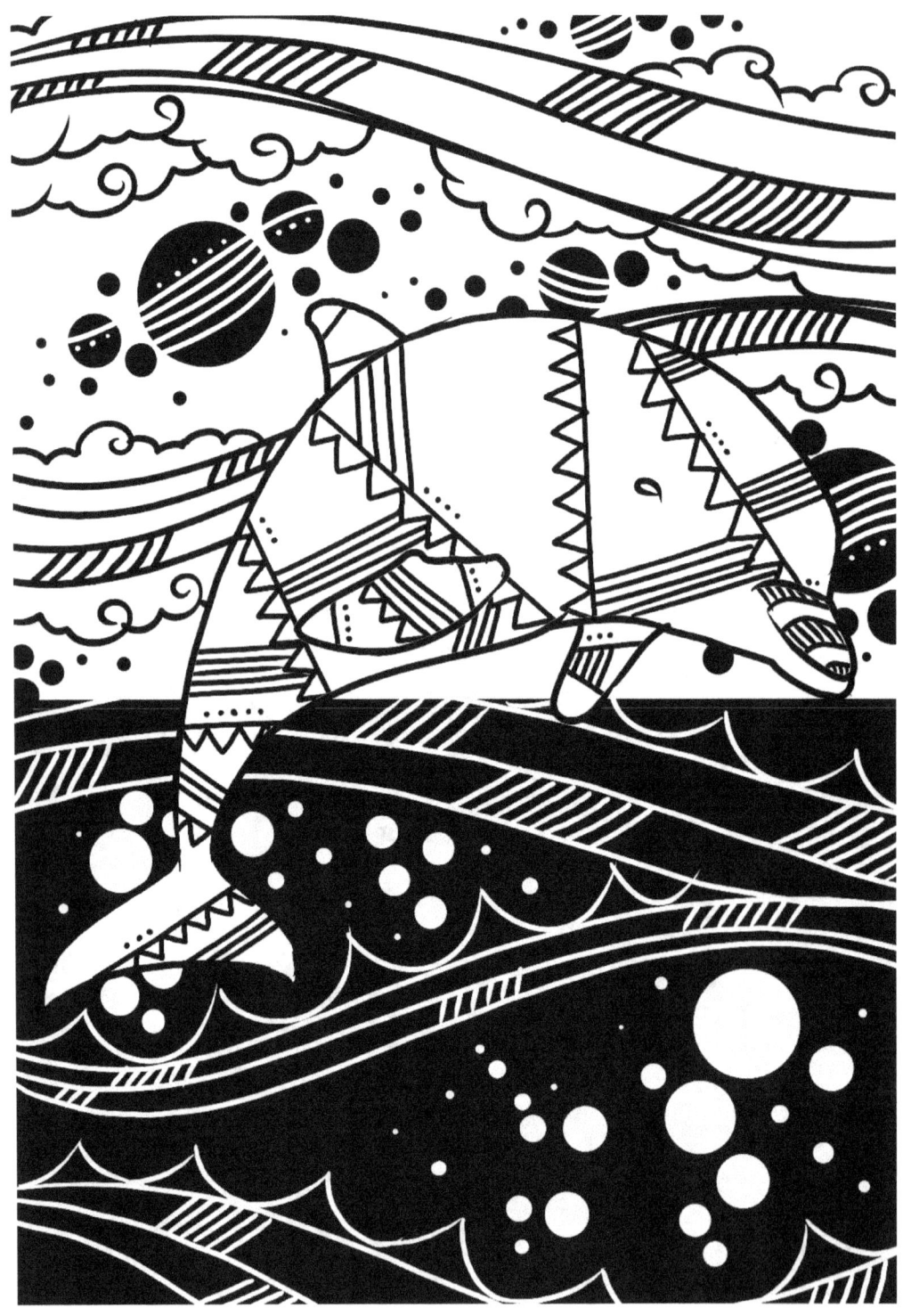

Doodle 7 – Lion

This being the final image, is also the most elegant of the images, as well as being the most unique of the previous doodles. In this one we start out with the casual lines and then begin shading almost instantly, as well as shading in the pattern too. This is something we have done very little of so far, but here's as good a time as any to give it a good college try! Carry on with this doodle by utilizing the next three images, and make sure you watch you're shading, smudging at this point is easy if you're using hands on tools so caution is advised.

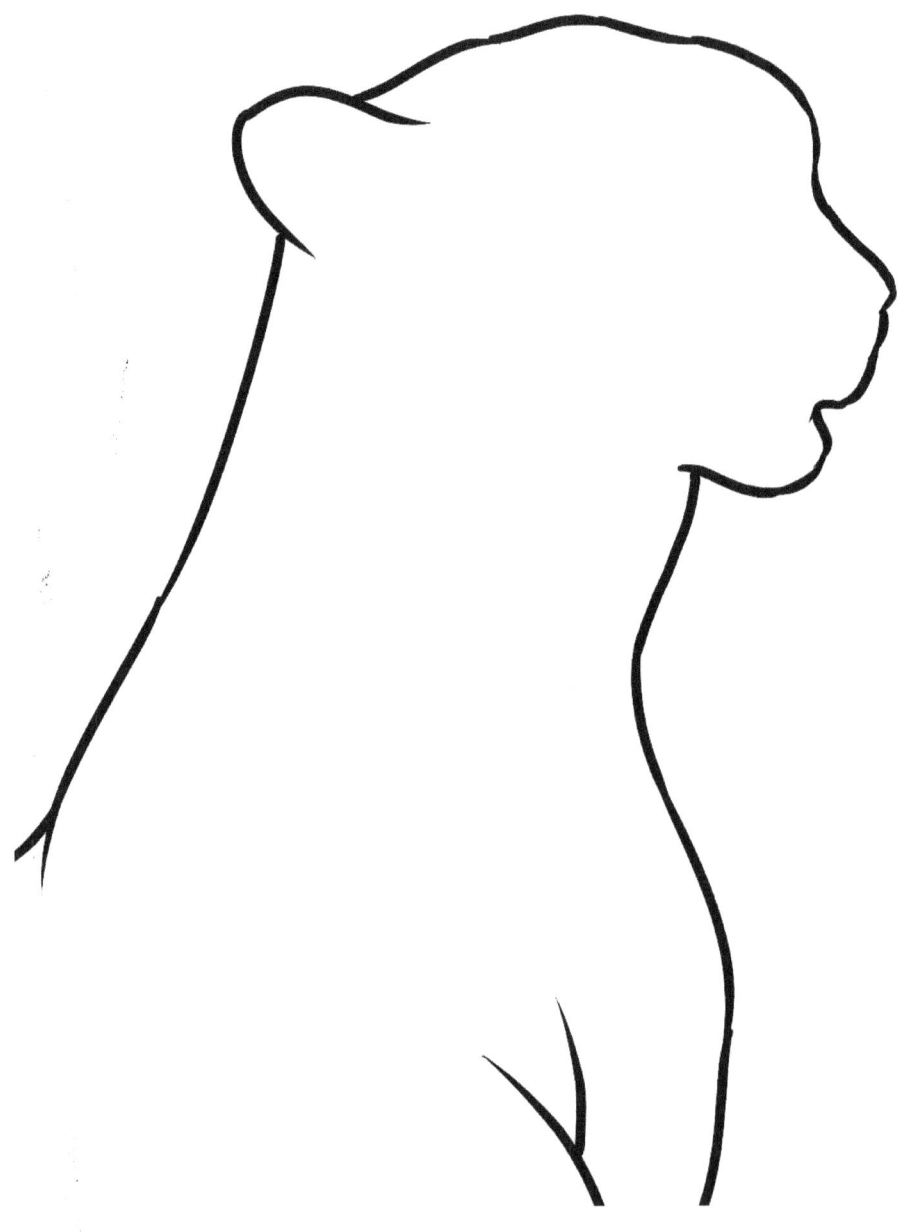

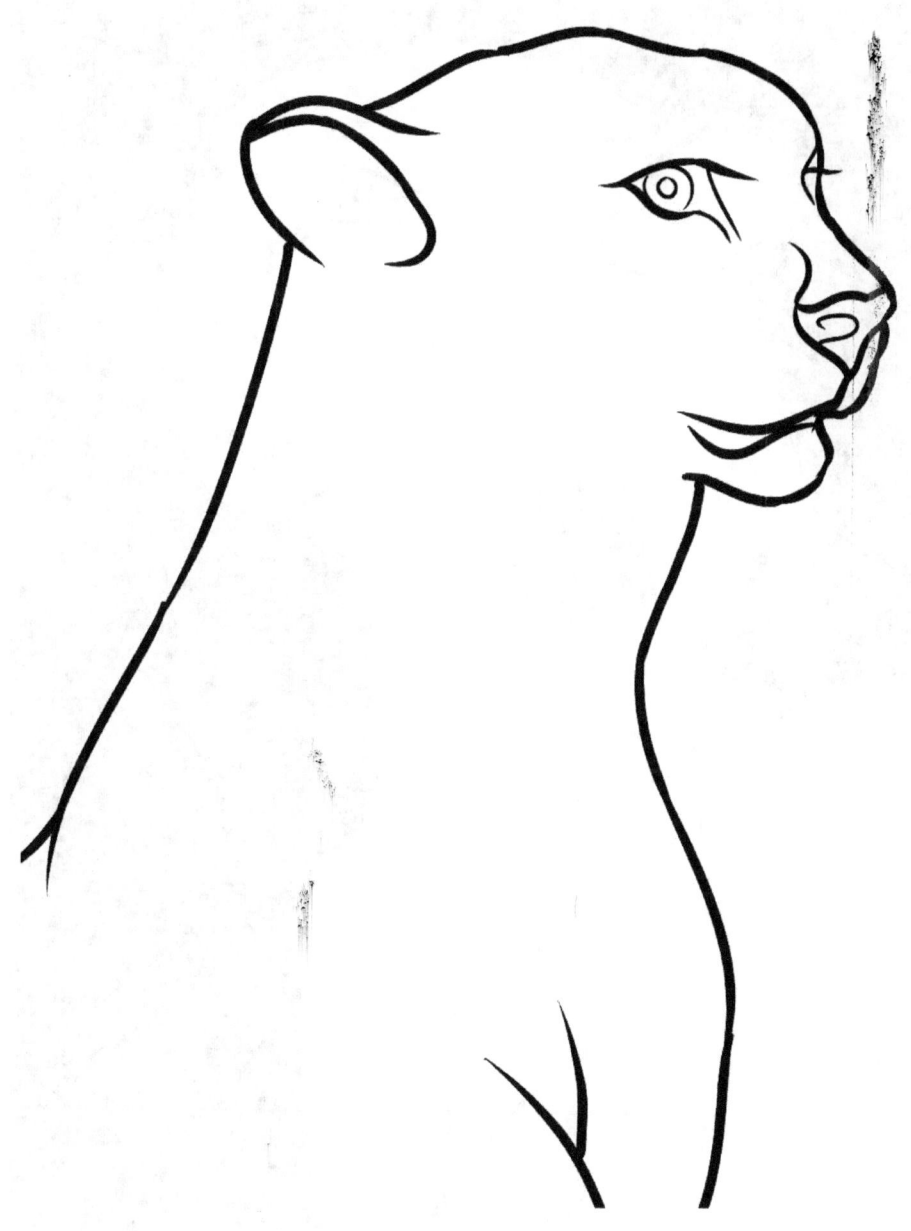

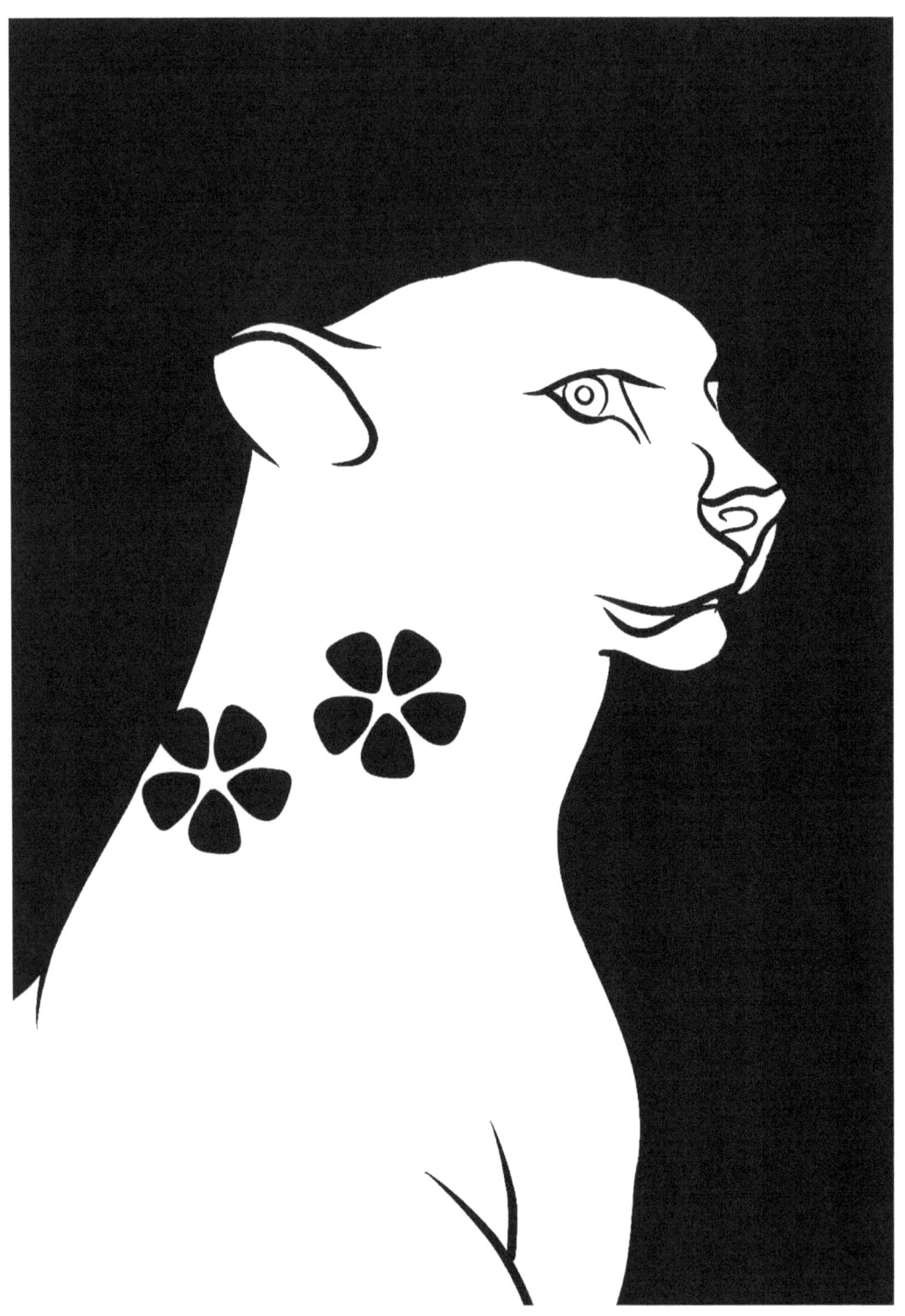

Now that you've made it through to the final set of images, you can really see how unique and specific this doodle is. You have such a remarkable use of light and dark in this set to create a stunning visual filled with rich patterns and design. This is amazing work and you should be proud of yourself for accomplishing it. Now you're free to create your own doodles using the knowledge you've gained here. Congratulations!

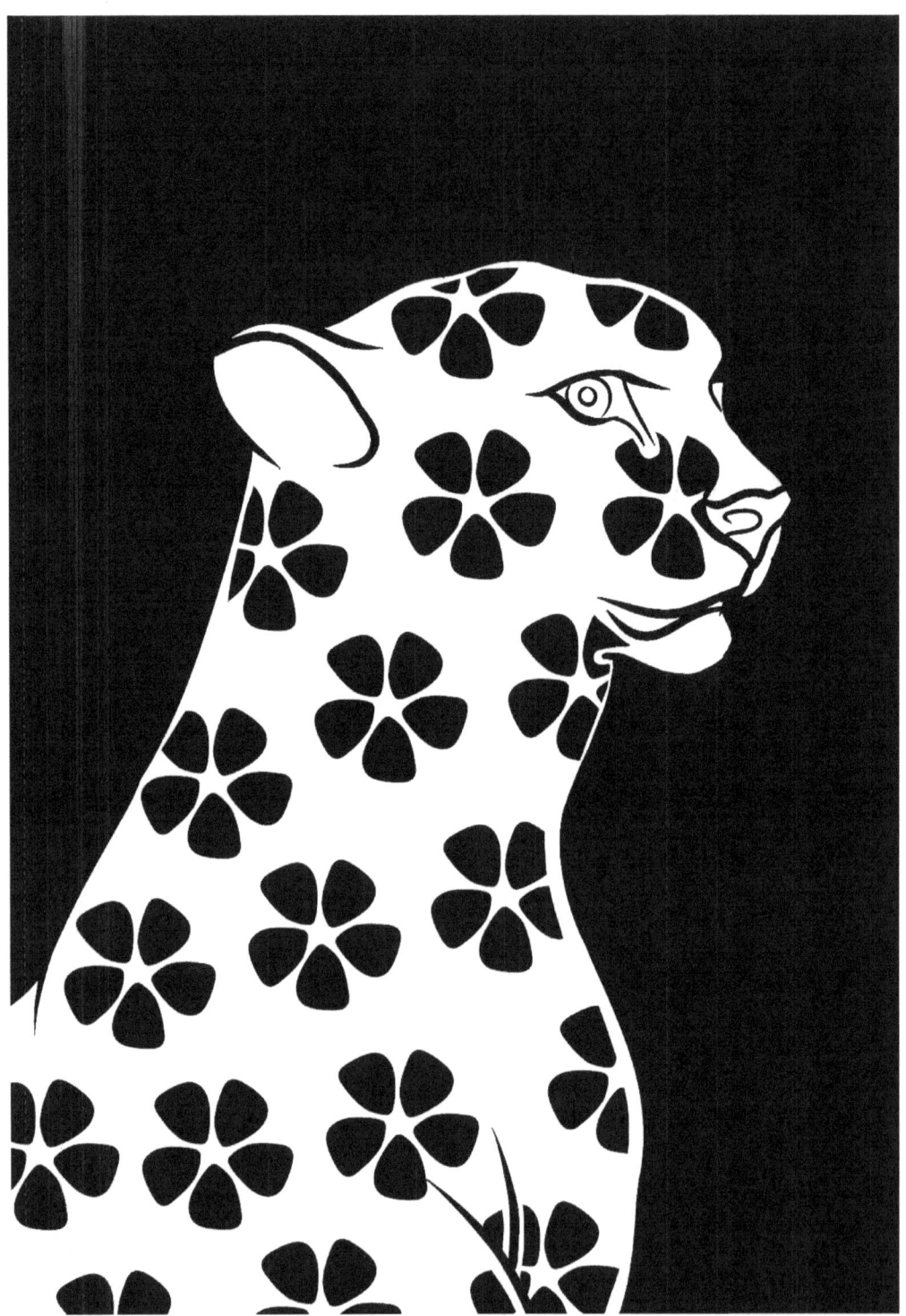

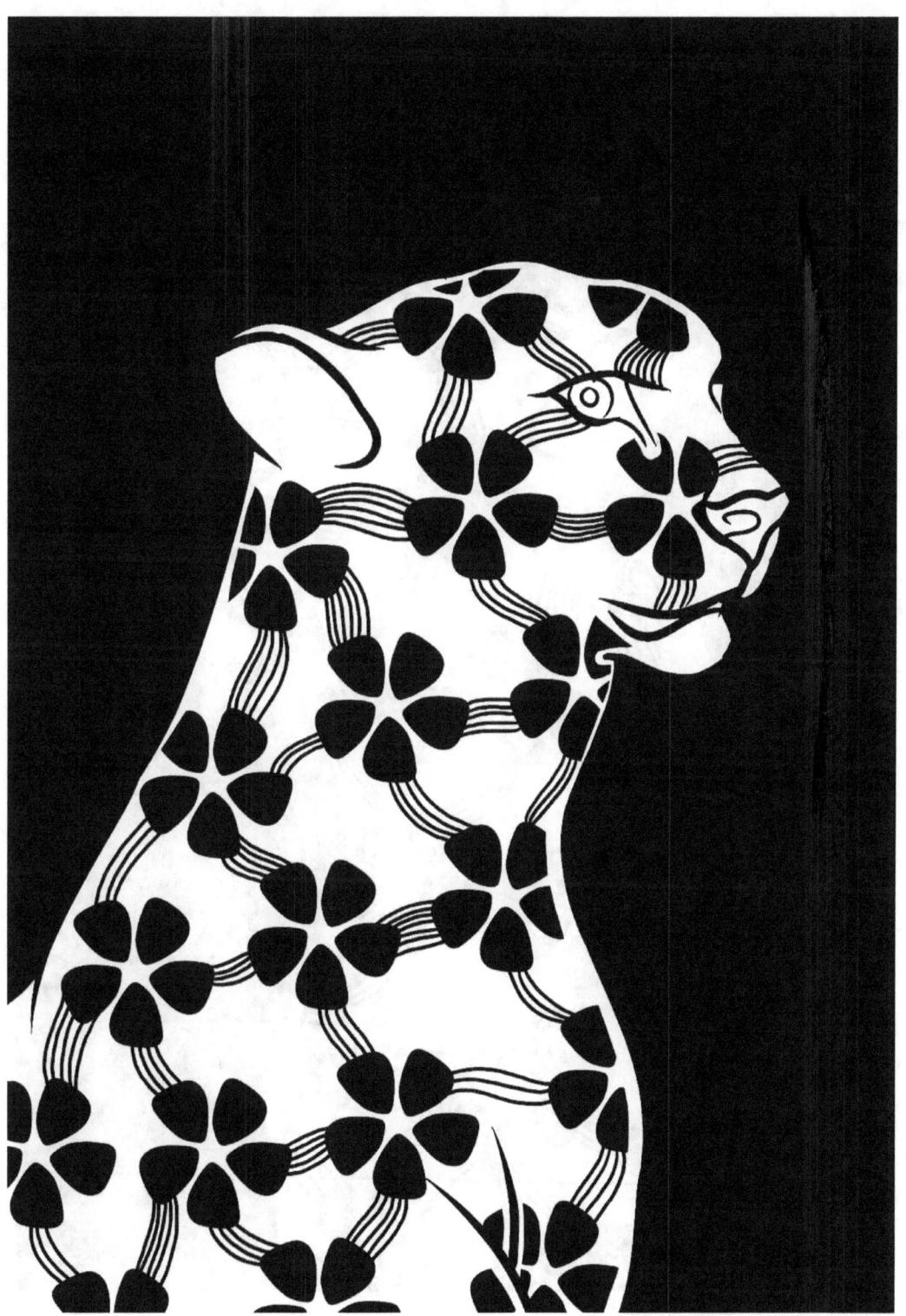

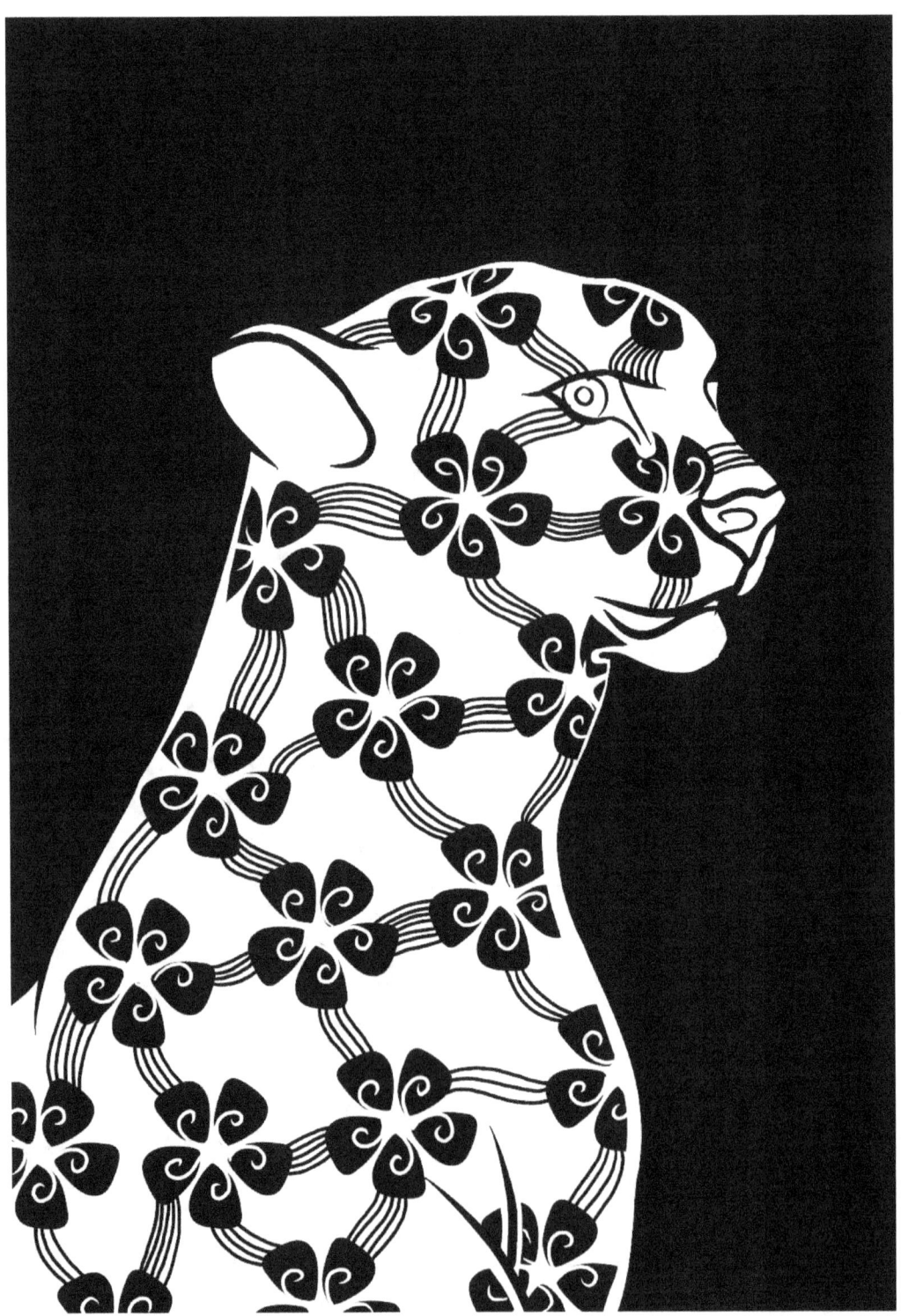

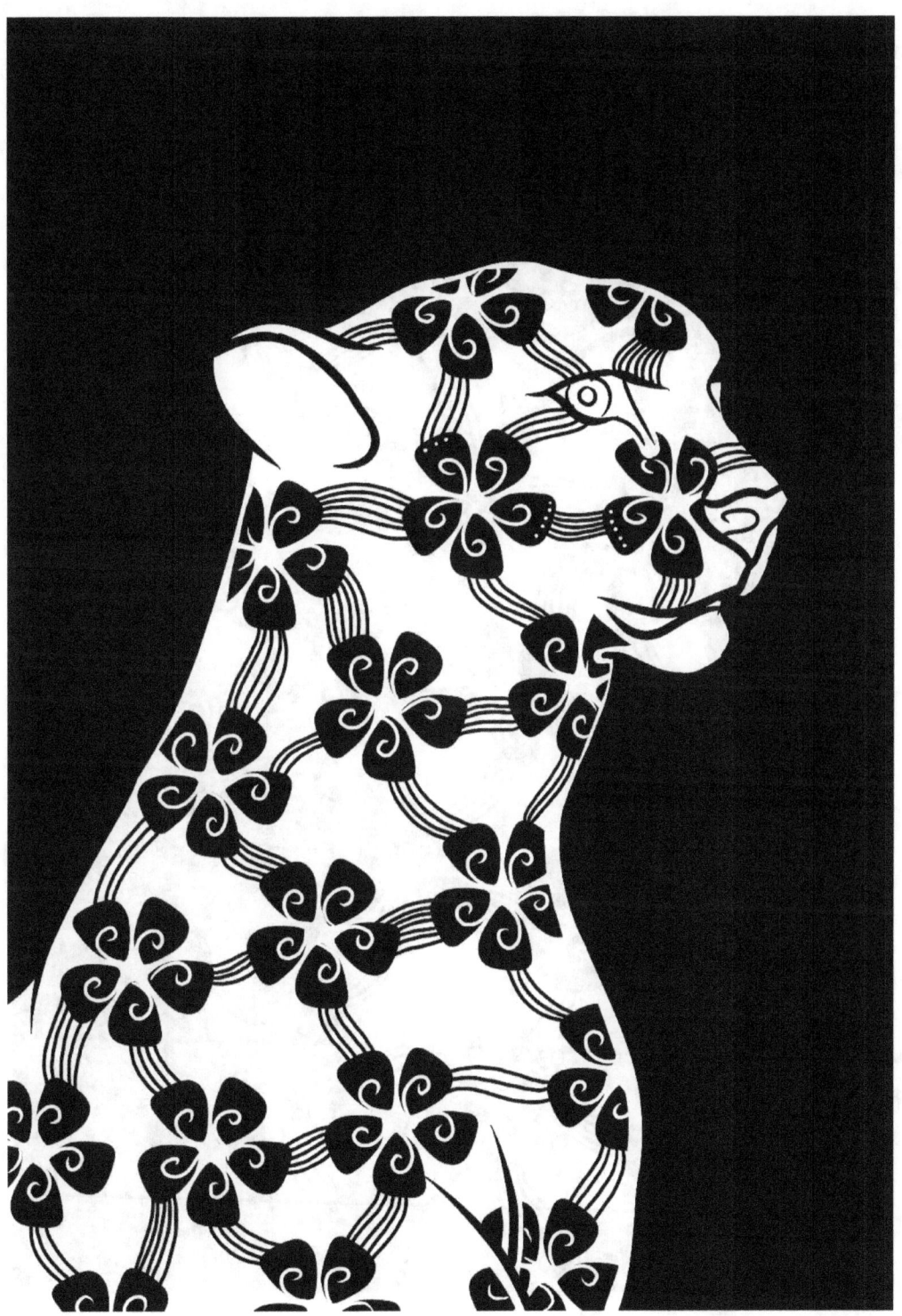

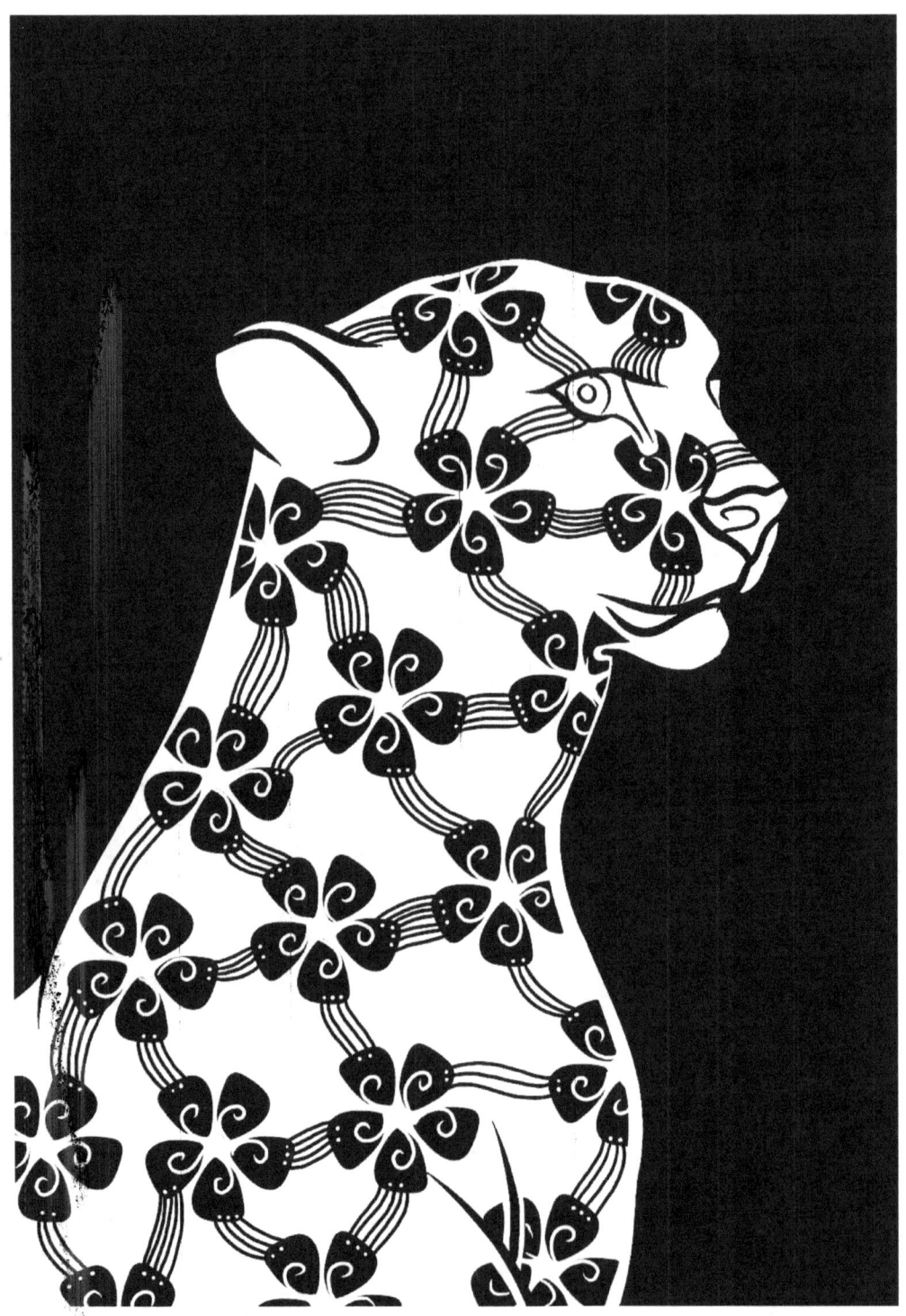

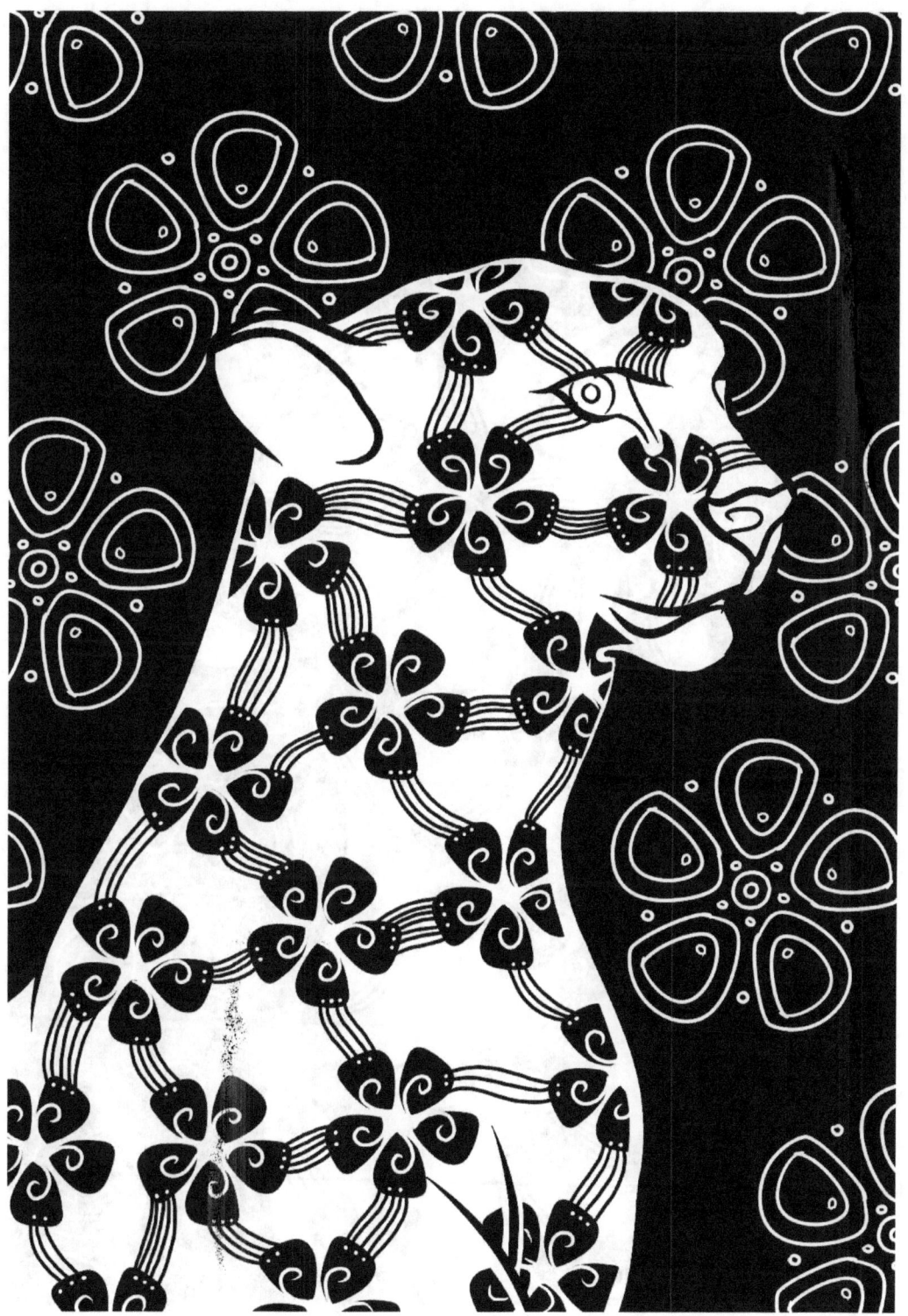

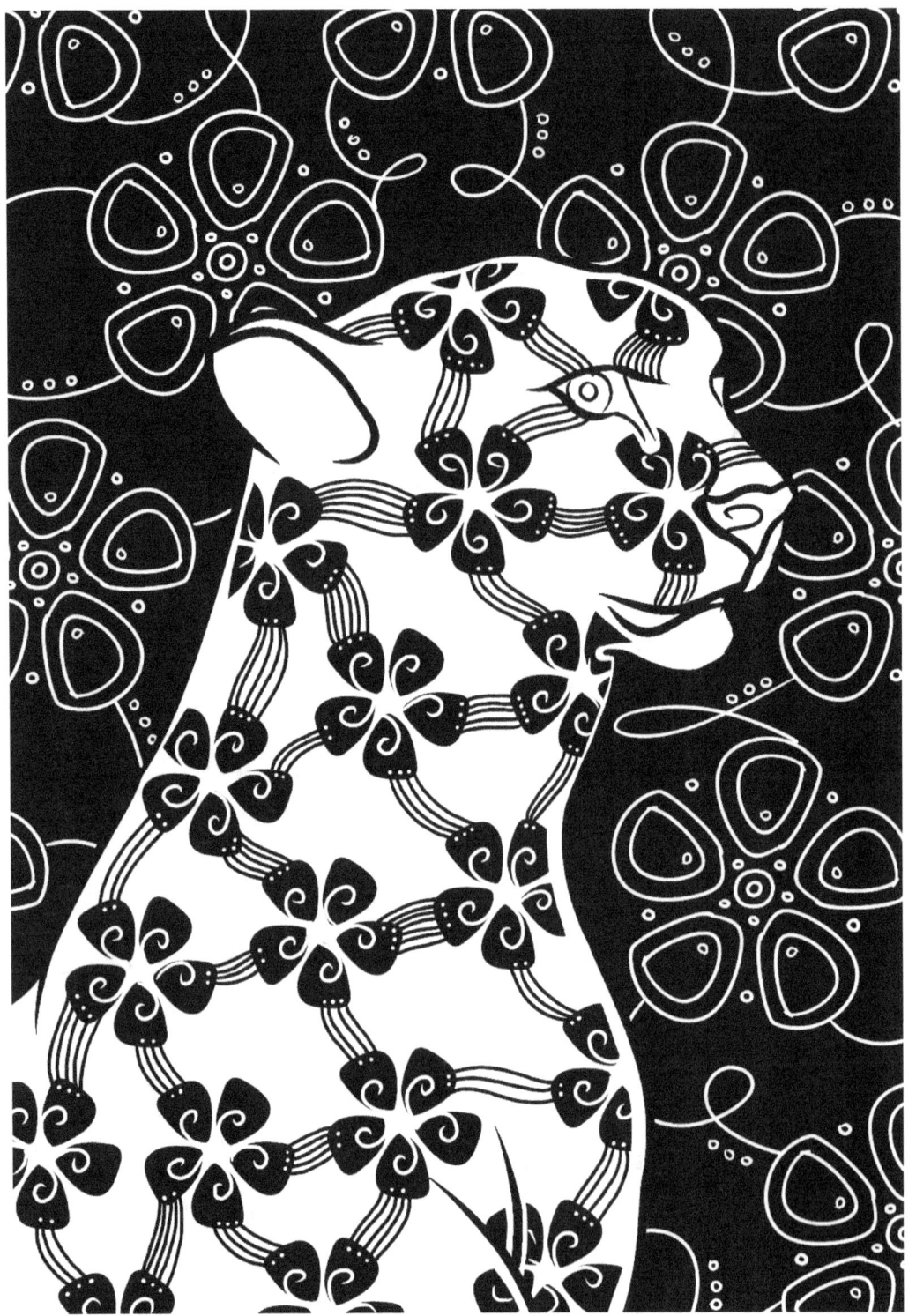

Conclusion

Well there you have it folks! That's all she wrote! You've now successfully completed the process of learning twenty new patterns and starting and completing 7 unique and full doodles. A very impressive feat that you should definitely brag about, go get started on that! Before you go though, take a second to appreciate all that you learned from these pages and the tools you'll have available for your future artistic endeavors. While these patterns are taken directly from Zen doodles specifically, I would say you have the ability to apply them to whatever you feel like creating. As well as the doodles themselves, take advantage of what you know and use it as often as you wish. Make art for friends; decorate your home or your office. Anything is possible and you're an unstoppable force of creativity. Go celebrate your finished work!

To download free bonus templates please follow the link below:

https://drive.google.com/open?id=
0B2v1XmtQAtt6cWticjcycm1qOXM

If you have some problems with downloading please contact me:

gloria.kemer@gmail.com

Thank you!

Thank you for choosing our book, we hope you found it interesting and helpful.

If you liked the book, please give us a favor to write your review.

We would really appreciate this!

If you would like to have a bonus – **FREE BOOK**, please send the screenshot of your review to this e-mail:

gloria.kemer@gmail.com and we will send you a **FREE BOOK** in PDF as a **GIFT!****

Hope to see you in our future books and good luck in your drawing experience!

** in the e-mail subject please mention the name of the book you reviewed and the author.

www.ingramcontent.com/pod-product-compliance
Lightning Source LLC
Chambersburg PA
CBHW080249180526
45167CB00006B/2466